A Kiss for the Absolute

The Lockert Library of Poetry in Translation

SERIES EDITORS
Peter Cole, Richard Sieburth, and Rosanna Warren

SERIES EDITOR EMERITUS (1991–2016)
Richard Howard

For other titles in the Lockert Library, see the list at the end of this volume.

A Kiss for the Absolute

SELECTED POEMS OF SHUZO TAKIGUCHI

Translated by Mary Jo Bang and Yuki Tanaka

PRINCETON UNIVERSITY PRESS
PRINCETON AND OXFORD

Published by Princeton University Press

41 William Street, Princeton, New Jersey 08540

99 Banbury Road, Oxford OX2 6JX

press.princeton.edu

All Rights Reserved

ISBN 9780691263892

ISBN (pbk.) 9780691263885

ISBN (e-book) 9780691263878

British Library Cataloging-in-Publication Data is available

Editorial: Anne Savarese and James Collier

Production Editorial: Jaden Young

Text and Cover Design: Pamela L. Schnitter

Production: Lauren Reese

Publicity: Jodi Price and Carmen Jimenez

Copyeditor: Jennifer Harris

Jacket image: steeve-x-art / Alamy Stock Photo

The Lockert Library of Poetry in Translation is supported by a bequest from Charles Lacy Lockert (1888–1974)

This book has been composed in Minion Pro

10 9 8 7 6 5 4 3 2 1

CONTENTS

When *The Poetic Experiments of Shuzo Takiguchi 1927–37* was published in Japan in 1967, tucked inside the book-jacket flap was a small, single-sheet, accordion-pleated appendix that began, "An other inside me made me choose this kind of title. The editor is of course myself." That deferral to the "other inside me" recalls Arthur Rimbaud's famous statement: "Je est un autre" (I is an other). This Rimbaldian echo is Takiguchi's way of making it clear, with his "red-banded sardonyx wit," that the "I" in these poems should not be read as autobiographical, but as a constructed poetic entity—an impish shape-shifter who dashes quickly through a world overflowing with associative imagery and who hops from one literary, scientific, or philosophical allusion to another, speaks multiple languages, and has a penchant for comical puns. The resulting high-voltage poems appear to leap over Modernism and land with both feet firmly planted in a prescient postmodern sensibility. For all their slippery indeterminacy, the poems are also deeply political, rooted in ideas about artistic freedom, the freedom of the imagination, and especially the freedom to be one's self in spite of a steady undercurrent of imminent peril. It's rather astonishing that these poems were written nearly a hundred years ago. In "The Cactus Brothers," he teasingly writes, "Ye probably don't know me yet." We can never know Takiguchi, he died in 1979. His poems, however, provide a window through which we can glimpse the workings of his inimitable mind.

Takiguchi was born in 1903 into an educated, civic-minded family in Toyama Prefecture, a northern alpine area on the Japan Sea coast. As the only son (with two older sisters), he was expected to follow in the footsteps of his father, and his grandfather, and become a physician. However, in April 1923, when he first arrived in Tokyo and enrolled at Keio University, he chose aesthetics as his area of study. Later, he would say he'd been bored by the lectures, choosing to read William Blake in the original English in the library instead of attending classes. It is impossible to know what he might have become had he continued on that academic path, because at 11:58 a.m. on September 1, 1923, the Great Kanto Earthquake occurred. The quake was followed by a 40-foot tsunami and fires throughout the city; Tokyo was nearly destroyed. Takiguchi says he grabbed *News from Nowhere* by William Morris (a utopian socialist novel published in 1890) and walked the streets. A local vigilante group, finding his long hair suspicious, chased him with a bamboo spear. His sister encouraged him to join her in Hokkaido, where he hoped to get a job as a teacher. In any event, he was not successful. In his "Chronology," he writes, "I was determined to devote my life to teaching children, but couldn't find a job and felt bad living the life of a freeloader." In 1924, he and his two sisters devised a plan to open a stationery and crafts shop. The following year, the store opened, but his sister begged him to go back to school as an investment in the future.

As a result, in April 1925, against his better judgment, he went back to Keio University. There, he became part of a coterie surrounding Junzaburo Nishiwaki, a poet and classicist who had studied English literature at Oxford University and had a deep interest in all things European and American, the more up to date the better. Under the influence of Nishiwaki, whose favorite poet was John Keats, Takiguchi was introduced to French Surrealism and began to write poems. In 1927, the small group of Nishiwaki acolytes founded a journal, *Fukuikutaru Kafu Yo: Collection Surréaliste* (O Fragrant Stoker: Surrealist Collection). Although only one issue of the journal was published, it spawned other surrealist magazines. In a later essay, "Chogenjitsushugi to watashi no shiteki taiken" (Surrealism and My Poetic Experience), Takiguchi writes that when he left the university after the earthquake, he sold all of his literature books; upon his return, it was surrealist thinking that "punched through that void."

Once it was introduced, Surrealism quickly became the dominant avant-garde practice among young poets in Japan. The ideas behind it—privileging spontaneity and chance over the restrictive conventions of the past—had tremendous appeal. It became a signifier not just of youthful rebellion but also of a sustained resistance to the Socratic "unexamined life." Takiguchi devoted himself to both documenting Surrealism and adapting it to his language and culture. While writing and doing his course work, he also translated the work of the French Surrealists Louis Aragon, André Breton, and Paul Éluard. In 1930, he published his translation of Breton's 1928 *Le surréalisme et la peinture* (*Surrealism and Painting*). He also wrote to Breton, initiating a relationship that would continue for years.

Takiguchi, however, did more than simply adopt the surrealist mode of writing dream-like, image-driven poems. Fueled by avant-garde bravado, and his extraordinary, wry intelligence, he embeds complex ideas in meticulous patterns of wordplay. By exploiting the natural ambiguity of language and skipping between the literal and figurative meanings of words, he effectively pushes a reader's mind in multiple directions. To fully appreciate everything that is being said, the reader is required to rapidly dismantle each term—whether a Japanese character or an English, French, or Latin phrase that he has incorporated into the poem—and then reassemble the language in a manner that suggests something new. With each dismantling and reconstruction, a single meaning becomes multiple possible meanings and more and more sense is made, and more pleasure is derived. This strategy becomes an argument about how language works, about how poetry works, and especially about how the imagination works.

Takiguchi's poems are a celebration of, and argument for, fluidity of every kind, including gender fluidity. Eros is not only an abiding theme in his poems but the erotic potential of even what seems like non-erotic language becomes an engine that keeps turning the rhetorical surface of the poems into a game of chance where words bump up against each other and send off sparks. Chance is both a symbolist and surrealist trope, but Takiguchi's poems further compound the sense of the accidental. He sometimes metapoetically addresses his own strategies, another practice that places him squarely in the postmodernist era:

> Her faint mustache speaks of a natural disaster in the
> Country of Wax. She is moving back and forth, com-
> ing and going, in a lipstick lens that is burning up time.
> The secret of personal pronouns. The sensation of time.

O traces of time that drastically change the interior of
my six-sided room, the way snow would. A bed of light
born inside a slipped-off sable stole. Her swoon assumes
an eternal oval. The beautiful game where one mistakes
water for land will soon come to an end.

—from "A Kiss for the Absolute"

Today, surrealism is no longer considered a radical strategy
but is, instead, a common element of both mainstream poetry
and commercial advertising; singing Amazon boxes and a talk-
ing gecko that advertises insurance are but two recent examples
of the latter. Takiguchi's poems make the practice of surrealist
defamiliarization more than a momentary distraction from the
mundane. His insights, although expressed in extravagant lan-
guage and delivered with cheeky impudence, are carefully con-
sidered. His poems are a mirror of his expansive personality,
verbal facility, and vast erudition: dadaist, surrealist, multilin-
gual (Japanese, French, English, as well as some Latin), indebted
to a multinational literary and artistic past, and deeply commit-
ted to positioning poetry at the intersection of philosophy and
modern psychology. The range of cultural references he includes
in the poems is striking. He gives us, to list only a few: Plato;
Botticelli; Venus; Tristan Tzara; Immaculate Mary; Cleopatra's
daughter; Mont Blanc; biblical King David (via an olive floun-
der that has David's bearded profile); Leda; "a polar bear OUI";
corned beef; the surrealist writers Paul Éluard and Louis Ara-
gon; and the artists Yves Tanguy, Max Ernst, Pablo Picasso, René
Magritte, Joan Miró, Man Ray, and Salvador Dalí. He includes
innumerable others, sometimes by name, sometimes by inge-
nious indirection.

*

In the twelfth century, translation referred to the moving of reliquary elements of a saint's body from one place to another. Written language in the Middle Ages was primarily the domain of the clergy and much clerical writing was about the lives of the saints. It makes sense that the word for carrying a saint's bones might in time be used for the act of carrying a work (about saints) written in one language over into another language. The transfer of language, however, is even more complicated than the delicate task of moving the remains of a body.

The transnational aspect of Takiguchi's work—his incorporation of multiple languages, in both the text and the titles of poems, and his expansive use of cultural and scientific allusion and various geographies—means that his poems rest on many pillars. In "Document d'Oiseaux: Documenting Birds," for example, Takiguchi writes: "The air is an exquisite boneless princess. She's Our Lady inside the straw. Gemstones are dropped like white roses into the PIAZZA of her throat. That white world was neither an isle nor an ibis." In Japanese, Italian, and English, Our Lady is, of course, the Madonna. That the throat of this Madonna has an Italian PIAZZA in it, confirms her relationship to Italy. The purity of the Madonna is associated with the color white, but here it is neither an isle nor a bird.

The fact that the gemstones are "like white roses" might make them pearls, a gem associated with Japan since the beginning of the twentieth century, when they were first cultured in the sea surrounding Ise-Shima. Both pearls and white roses have traditionally been associated with Mary, who is called "the Mystical Rose of Heaven." She is also associated with straw, having laid the newborn Christ child "in a manger"—an animal feed trough (Luke 2:7). The "straw" in Takiguchi's poem, however, is a drinking straw. The Column of the Immaculate Conception on the Piazza Mignanelli in Rome might be imagined by a Surrealist as a gigantic drinking straw. In this way, Takiguchi's poems create strange new worlds in which mythologies from different eras and geographies coexist.

In addition to the many multinational allusions, Takiguchi frequently uses puns, many of which defy translation. One example is his frequent punning on his own two-character name. The first character of his name means "waterfall," the second means "source" or "mouth." To echo Takiguchi's recurrent gesturing to his name, we formatted "LINES"—the poem Takiguchi himself titled in English—into the shape of an "S," for Shuzo. We felt encouraged to do this by Takiguchi's response to Hiroaki Sato, who had written to him with questions about how to translate aspects of this poem and several others in the 1970s:

> How to translate this into English (European language) is something that should be dealt with by writing style because I wanted to emphasize the uniqueness of Japanese by mixing in the author's subjectivity. Based on this premise, I'm not sure yet whether there is any method of creating a certain kind of visual, etc, effect in a European language. Italics? or Gothic? or—a style that uses no capital letters?*

* "Answers to 'A Set of Questions'—Occasional Brief Parenthetical Asides," *Collection Shuzo Takiguchi*, supplementary volume, p. 158 (Tokyo: Misuzu Shobo, 1998).

We gestured to the "T" in Takiguchi's name in the poem "Max Ernst" by translating 肉片 (scraps of meat) as "bits of T-bone" ("Night tourists / gobble up / night's cryptic handcuffs / as if they were bits of T-bone") and in "TEXTE ÉVANGÉLIQUE," we translated a "rose" as a tea rose, which we wrote as "T-rose" ("Please place that T-rose on my shoulder in yesterday's retro photo").

We tried throughout to capture the distinctive way Takiguchi uses language in the poems—especially the way he emphasizes duality. We continually examined his word choices, syntax, sound, grammar, and cultural and literary allusions, as well as the history of his era and the ways in which he cleverly encoded his preoccupations and obsessions. When there was no way to create an equivalency in English, we would sometimes create wordplay elsewhere to maintain the same level of play as occurs in the original. In "The Flower Basket Filled with Human Death," for example, Takiguchi uses the same scrap of meat (肉片) that he used in "Max Ernst"; since the piece of meat was now being eaten by a lion, on this occasion we translated the meat as "tenderloin" ("When that graceful god collided with a seven-string zither, it vanished like a scrap of tenderloin off a lion's palate").

*

When Takiguchi graduated from Keio University in 1931, he went to work for Photo Chemical Laboratories (PCL)—a newly established film company—as a scriptor, one who ensures continuity across scenes. He continued to write poems and to translate the Surrealists and became increasingly involved in the visual arts, especially photography. In January 1935, he met Ayako Suzuki at a gallery opening in Ueno; they married in December. In 1937, Takiguchi, along with Chiruu Yamanaka (known as Tiroux) organized the Exhibition of International Surrealist

Works in Japan, a major exhibition of surrealist art from abroad that began in Tokyo and then traveled to Kyoto, Osaka, Nagoya, and Fukui. It included work by Hans Arp, Hans Bellmer, André Breton, Giorgio de Chirico, Salvador Dalí, Marcel Duchamp, Paul Éluard, Max Ernst, Alberto Giacometti, Paul Klee, René Magritte, Joan Miro, Henry Moore, Pablo Picasso, Man Ray, and others. The two also edited an exhibition catalogue titled *Album Surréaliste*.

Between 1938 and early 1941, Takiguchi's art criticism included articles about Freud and contemporary art; about how the close-up in Japanese photography was indebted to cinema, especially to Luis Buñuel's 1929 film *Un Chien Andalou* (An Andalusian Dog) and others by Man Ray; about the surrealist relationship to objects, including Eugène Atget's objects in shop windows; about the Bauhaus artist Laszlo Moholy-Nagy's "Fotoplastiks"; and about the work of numerous other photographers, including Atget (French), Paul Nash (British), Edward Weston (American), and Hans Bellmer (German). In 1940, he published an article about his correspondence with Moholy-Nagy, who had immigrated to Chicago in 1937 to found a design school.

Outside the narrow world of poetry and art, worrisome changes were taking place. In the 1930s, the military had gained more power in the Japanese government, moving the country toward an expansionist policy in Asia. In 1937, the Second Sino-Japanese War broke out. As the war continued, daily life began to change. The government criticized luxury while praising the virtue of suffering poverty to win the war. Essentials such as gasoline and sugar came to be tightly controlled under a system of rationing. In a timeline that Takiguchi later constructed about his life, he writes of an event that occurred in 1940:

The first exhibit of the Art Culture Association took place, but it was already a dark time, there was sense of foreboding on the faces of the painters. The people around me felt the weight of the Special Higher Police and Intelligence Agency closing in on them. I felt both conflicted and isolated. I could feel the growing sense of a collapse of the surrealist vision and a sense of personal failure. In early winter, I coughed up blood from a stomach ulcer again. A certain friend came by and said I had completely missed the boat.*

On March 5, 1941, Takiguchi was arrested by the Tokubetsu Koto Keisatsu (shortened to Tokko), the Special Higher Police, now referred to as the "thought police." In the chronology, he describes the day:

On March 5, around 7:00 a.m., three Tokko police came to our house when we were still asleep. I asked them to wait until we finished breakfast. We cooked and ate rice and miso soup and made the police wait for an hour. They searched the house and confiscated about three hundred pieces of evidence such as magazines. I was taken to a police cell. I was interrogated once a week. After a month, they allowed for lunch to be sent in from the outside and I remember seeing cherry blossoms on the street from the police room. The focus of the interrogation was whether the Japanese Surrealist movement was in any way related to the International Communist Party (of course, there

* "Shuzo Takiguchi: Autobiographical Chronology and Addendum," *Collection Shuzo Takiguchi*, vol. 1, pp. 494–495 (Tokyo: Misuzu Shobo, 1991).

was no such thing) and other issues. They found an article about my correspondence with Breton in one of the confiscated magazines and interrogated me about that. I told my wife to hide these letters, so they escaped a second search. Being completely unable to grasp how much of a rippling effect this incident might have on others, I made every effort to take a passive stance. I was exhausted after the psychological threats and intimidation. Once I'd been admitted to my cell, I was assigned the role of handyman, which improved my health. That summer, they interrogated me again, but when I tried to approach the relationship between Surrealism and politics logically, the exchange became chaotic and even the young prosecutors looked confused. It was an irresolvable problem within myself.*

Takiguchi was held for eight months, along with the surrealist painter Ichiro Fukuzawa, for being a "thought criminal," a category that included anyone influenced by the West. The two men were both released from separate detention centers on November 11, 1941. Takiguchi writes that when he was released, he was warned by the police that he had better "be more careful in the future." The effect of the incarceration, and the ominous warning, appears to have been chilling. After his release from prison, Takiguchi wrote few poems that rise to the level of those in *Poetic Experiments* going on instead to become a visual artist, a major art critic, an exhibition curator, and a champion of

---

* "Shuzo Takiguchi: Autobiographical Chronology and Addendum," *Collection Shuzo Takiguchi*, vol. 1, p. 495 (Tokyo: Misuzu Shobo, 1991).

avant-garde art. He helped revive the avant-garde scene in post-war Japan by spearheading an interdisciplinary group called Jikken Kobo ("Experimental Workshop") that was active from 1951 to 1957; the group included not only painters but also the composer and music theorist Toru Takemitsu. He represented Japan at the Venice Biennale in 1958, afterward traveling to Spain—where he visited Dalí at home and also met Duchamp, who happened to be there—then to Paris where he finally met Breton in person at his storied apartment on rue Fontaine. In the late 1960s and 1970s, Takiguchi collaborated with Joan Miró on two books of poems and paintings. His collected works in Japanese, published posthumously between 1991 and 1998, number fourteen volumes. They include his art criticism, his writings on photography and Surrealism, his dream journals, his correspondence, and the contents of the book *The Poetic Experiments of Shuzo Takiguchi 1927–1937*. The book, published in 1967, is no longer in print but continues to have a cult following in Japan. While some of the short poems have been translated into English, primarily in the early 1970s by Hiroaki Sato, there has never been an English-language translation of many of the long prose poems, nor of the entire book. For *A Kiss for the Absolute: Selected Poems*, we chose those poems that best showcase Takiguchi's formal range, as well as his intrepid use of language and ingenious rhetorical conceits.

Having now enjoyed an inspiring and productive relationship with Shuzo Takiguchi for these past ten years, we are very happy to be able to introduce him to English-speaking readers. At the end of "The Royal Family of Dreams: A Manifesto, or Regarding A Priori Dreams," Takiguchi writes:

On the eve of an endless revolution, the ink of my mind is drenched with dream colors. The headwind of an unassailable dream flutters my lashes. O animals of objectivity high in the sky, O snail-gray monotony, try as you might to measure me. Try as you might to love me.

That is also our hope as translators, that readers encountering this poet and his poems will love both as much as we do.

Mary Jo Bang, St. Louis, Missouri
Yuki Tanaka, Tokyo, Japan

A Kiss for the Absolute

LINES

赤イウロコノ魚ガ巧ミニ衝突スル街路ニ
顔ヲヒソマセテイルト
精密ナ息切レノ内部デ
花ガ重タク
虎ハ離レル

葦ハ
クラリネットノ煩悶ヲスル
真珠貝ニ気附イテイル夕立雲ヲ
傾斜ニ変更シテ

凹ンダ少女ガ朝ノ街ニユラユラシテイル
ムラサキノ硝子ヲワクワクサセナガラ
薔薇ノ花瓣ニ放火シテ
ボティチェリノ少年ヲ慕ッタ記憶ガ
金メッキノ花飾ニツメヨル
彼女ノ黒子ハ微風ヲ起スホド青イ

LINES

red-plated fish skillfully collide head-on in the intersection,

that's when the face gets hidden

in a fine-tuned gasping

a rose becomes weighty and downcast

and the tigress splits

the reed makes a deal

with the clarinet's ordeal

changing the inclination

of evening showers that know what's up with a pearl shell

on the morning streets a dented girl moves side to side

exciting purple glass

setting fire to rose petals

memories of longing for the Botticelli boy

pressing in on her gilt-floral chaplet

her beauty-mark mole is so blue it shakes the wind awake.

クレオパトラの娘の悪事

　朝になると凍る湖水のほとりでアントニオとクレオパトラとが世界でもっとも精確な時計を愛する。　彼らは誰れ誰れに似ているか。　彼らは結婚したものであり雛菊の香を嗅いでみた最初の文明人である。　均衡を欠いたために崩れた美しい湖畔のホテルがある。　それはホテル自身の殊勲であった。　クレオパトラは水泳の非常に達者な母親であった。ぼくは椿事の写真を信じるように彼女を信じる。　けれどもこの運動はほんとうに有効であるのかクレオパトラよ。　馬鹿げた蛙の體内に飛び込んだ天使の勇気は永遠の謎に終る。ぼくはギリシャの円柱を信じないように彼らの言葉を信用しない。　けれども真理は微風のようにやってきた。　やはりクレオパトラは美人であった。　華やかな夕日がクレオパトラを照らした。　その夜遅くようやくクレオパトラの娘から手紙が届いたのである。

　——わたくしはきのう孔雀の姿にあなたの影を見た。嵐が来たためにそれは消えたけれど砂漠の雪の遺跡を遊歩する

The Misdeeds of Cleopatra's Daughter

Next to a lake that freezes each morning at dawn, Antony and Cleopatra are adoring the world's most accurate clock. Who do they remind you of? They're a married couple and the first civilized people to have smelled a daisy. There's a beautiful lakeside inn there that once lost its composure and collapsed. That very hotel had been commended and decorated. Cleopatra was a mother and an extremely skilled swimmer. I trust the snapshot of the startling incident as well as I trust her. But is this movement really helpful, Cleopatra? The daring of the angel who plunges into the body of a harebrained frog ends up being an unending mystery. Just as I don't place my trust in pillars in Greece, I don't rely on what they have to say. But then Truth breezed in. As I said, Cleopatra was a beautiful woman. A gorgeous sunset threw light on her: C=L=E=O=P=A=T=R=A. Later that same night, a letter finally arrived from Cleopatra's daughter.

"—Just yesterday I saw your shadowy outline in the shape of a peacock. It disappeared as a storm dragged in, but your soul went on endlessly singing as it wandered around in the ruins of the desert snow. When that whole idling engine was just a white

あなたの魂は永遠に歌っていた。　まどろむ機械が星空の白い雲であったとき、それは神の黄金よりも賢明であった。いま死んだばかりの蜉蝣は急いで花束を携えて飛来する。こうした空間での噴水が青空とわたくしの窓とのあいだで四十数片の砕片に引き裂かれて永遠に微笑んだのはわたくしの最初の悪事であった。　あなたの反対側にある大理石が綻びたときあなたも同じように微笑んだではないか。　装飾されつくした花束のようにもはや誰れも語らないであろう。しかしクレオパトラの娘は白く乾いた麦藁の内部に生れたものである。わたくしは盲目のように瞑った眼をして巡遊する。わたくしの休息は単一の太陽に驚く蓮華のなかでもっとも美しい蓮華である。　ああと叫ぶ声の木魂がやはりああであった室内に完全に眼覚めていた猫・熟睡する怒濤を訪ねてわたくしの顔を静かに鏡にうつす。　わたくしの眉は薔薇に平行する一匹の青藍色の魚が躍ねあがった翌日である。　それは永続する噴水の理性を要求する一少女わたくしである。　巨大な太陽がお辞儀する。　わたくしの優しい爪に映る幸運は混合した羊とエメラルドとであった。　わたくしはそれを信じている。　植物採集家が驚嘆したわたくしの扇のなかには深緑の呼吸がある。わたくしはそれを浮彫りされたギリシァ風の青白い月光の海岸で使用するのであるが、遠洋航海者たちがそれを打ち眺めながら通過する。　それは遥かな水平線上のめまぐるしい見物であった。彼らはわたくしを見ていた。　かの滑らかな濃藍の

cloud in the starry sky, it was still more informed than the gold of gods. The still-warm corpse of a mayfly comes flying in in a hurry with a bouquet. When, in the open space between the sky-blue sky and my window, a fountain was shattered into forty-odd bits, I smiled without end—that was my first misdeed. When the marble bust opposite you burst open at the seams, you smiled a little too, didn't you? Like an over-embellished bouquet, no one will simply speak anymore. But Cleopatra's daughter was born in a nest of pale dry straw. I go on tottering around with my eyes shut, as if I were blind. My beauty sleep is like that of the most beautiful lotus among lotuses amazed by the fact that there is a single sun. A visit to a wide-awake cat in a room where there were raving waves of deep sleep and where the echo of the shouted *Ah* was also an *aah* is where I quietly let my own face be reflected in a mirror. My eyebrows represent the day after one ultramarine fish leapt up parallel to a rose. It is I, a young girl, who demands a rationale for those enduring fountains. A giant sun takes a bow. The windfall reflected in my kindly fingernails was a compound of sheep and emerald. I trust in it. In my fanning palm frond, which stunned a plant collector, there is deep-green breath. I use it on the coastline in a Greek-style bas-relief of pale moonlight, and sailors stare at it as they pass. It always provided a dizzying spectacle on the distant horizon. They were

水面を刈っている喜劇役者がいる。　なんという美しい月夜であろう。　わたくしの窓を壊しにきた殺人犯よ。　わたくしを殺す前に眺めよ。　わたくしはそれを複雑な松の枝のあいだから望むことを許す。　時間と時間とのあいだのわたくしの容貌がなんとおまえに似ていることよ。

　全體が湖水である大理石の美神に寄り添って完全な果実を虚空から無限にすくい取るのは花火の過失である。　わたくしは青空の農業を知っている。　雲の形の鶏は星をついばんでいる。　それはエルサレムから程遠い野菜園であった。

　曙を傘にしたわたくしの卵のような指をよくごらん。　自働人形のような水仙の微細な心配をよくごらん。　わたくしは種子を播きながら昇天してしまった農夫の血色のいい顔を全部憶えている。　紫の怒濤がかの男に打ち寄せる。　それでも彼が煙草を喫っているのは彼の習性によるのでありわたくしが彼の肩に不意に刺繍して置くのは鶴の習性であった。わたくしに純枠な鶴が飛んできた。　わたくしは舞いながら眞珠貝の悪事を知っていた鶴のように優しい。　わたくしはわたくしの手と指のように美しい。あのもっとも美しい蓮華がわたくしに柔順であることはわたくしを絶えず新しくする。わたくしは何ものをも恐れない予定であった。わたくしは宮殿に坐った

watching me from afar. There's a comedian here who keeps busy shaving that smooth aquamarine surface of the water. What a beautiful moonlit night. You a manslayer who came to break in through my window. Look before you slay me. I'll let you watch between the intricate branches of a pine tree. How my features match yours from one time to another.

The mistake of the fireworks' display is to get too close to the marble Goddess of Beauty—whose entire body is a lake—and endlessly scoop perfect fruit out of the emptiness. I know the sky-blue sky's agriculture. A cloud-shaped hen keeps pecking at the stars. That was in a green garden far from Jerusalem.

Look closely at my yolky fingers that turned dawn into a parasol. Carefully examine the subtle anxiety of the narcissus that is acting like an automaton. I can still call to mind every detail of the florid face of that farmer who died and went to heaven while still sowing seeds. Purple waves rage and break over that man. Still and all he would smoke cigarettes because that was his habit and I would quickly needlework his shoulders because that was a crane's way. Once a pure crane flew right to me. I'm as gentle as the crane that danced all over the place while still grasping the misdeeds of the pearl oyster shell. I am beautiful, as are my hands and fingers. The fact that the loveliest lotus flowers bow down to me keeps renewing me. I had planned to not fear anything.

最新のカンガルーであった。　わたくしの母親は飛び去った天使であった‥‥‥

　　これが美人クレオパトラの娘の真理である。
　　これが湖上のもっとも古典的な通信である。
　　これが湖上の鶴のあくびである。

I was only the latest kangaroo to be seated at the palace.   My
mother was a perfect angel who flew off . . . "

This is the truth of the lovely Cleopatra's daughter.

This is the most classical exchange of letters on the lake.

This is a crane on the lake with its mouth open in a yawn.

五月のスフィンクス

見えない寝床の巨大な鳥
風の臓腑は美しく見える

★

夜光時計も飢えている
けちらされた星たちは
生命の動物たち
美しい女たち飢えたものたちは
遠い不可解の時間ののち
憑かれた虹から乳をのむ

★

夜のない星
盲いた眼の噴水
風の鏡のなかの巨大な夜々
透明な雛鳥の巨大な足跡

★

羞恥のない美のくぼみと自由
あなたはラジュームの果実である

The Sphinx in May

An immense bird on an invisible bed
The wind's viscera seem beautiful

★

A luminous watch is famished too
Kick-scattered stars
become life's animals
After a distant mystifying time
ravishing women famished things
gulp down milk from a possessed rainbow

★

Stars with no night
Fountains with blind oculi
Immense nights in the wind's mirror
Immense footprints of transparent chicks

★

The freedoms and hollows of unabashed beauty
You are a radium plum

しかしうら若いその手はすぐ
黒い無限の手袋に慣れるだろう

暴風の日に
ぼくたちは怖ろしい孤独の虹を
殺された砂の上で放牧するだろう

★

水は心臓を鳥は澄明をもつ

もっとも美しいものを逃がす人間の手
もっとも美しいものを殺す鳥たちの眼
自然のなかに地球のような
ひとつの美しい視線

★

恋人たち巨大な匂い明日そしてぼくは眠る
三角洲のなかの巨大な菫砂漠の診察
美しい燃える雨数えられない自由の鳥たち
抜錨した船ぼくは縮れ毛のある木炭を見る

★

But those young hands will soon become
used to infinite ebony gloves

On a day of tempestuous weather
we'll put out the rainbow of terrifying sadness
to graze on assassinated sand

★

Water has a heart, birds have clarity

Human hands that release the loveliest things
The eyes of birds that kill the loveliest things
In nature as on earth
one single sightline

★

Lovers the immense scent "Tomorrow . . . " and I'm out like
   a light
The clinical analysis of an immense violet desert in a delta
Beautiful burning rain countless liberated birds
I, a ship that weighed anchor, see charcoal with its frizzy hair

★

透明な水の千の企みのように
街の無数の曲り角にいる
濡れ羽色の乳房たち
誰れのためにも光らない星たち
空の花バラたちの苦痛
千の虹のピラミッド

★

黒い花園の貝殻の寝床
ぼくは裂かれた雨たちの音を聴く
曲った虹の青ざめた乳

★

貝殻この変った種子この幸運の鳥たちは
縮れ毛のある椅子で
夢を見るために笑った
永い永い薔薇の花から
顫音の撒水車を出すために笑った

永遠の電話のための美しい男根

Like the thousand tricks of transparent water
raven-dark hair feathering breasts
on countless street corners
Stars that shine for no one
The flower of the sky the pain of roses
A pyramid made of a thousand rainbows

★

A seashell's bed in a dark botanical garden
I listen to the sound of torn rain
The pale breasts of curved rainbows

★

A shell this odd seed these birds of fortune
laughed in order to dream
on a chair with curly hair
Laughed to send out a trilling street-sprinkler
from the rose that goes on and on

A lovely phallic tool for unending phone calls

絶対への接吻

　ぼくの黄金の爪の内部の瀧の飛沫に濡れた客間に襲来するひとりの純粋直観の女性。　彼女の指の上に光った金剛石が狩獵者に踏みこまれていたか否かをぼくは問わない。　彼女の水平であり同時に垂直である乳房は飽和した秤器のような衣服に包まれている。　蠟の国の天災を、彼女の仄かな髭が物語る。　彼女は時間を燃焼しつつある口紅の鏡玉の前後左右を動いている。　人称の秘密。　時の感覚。　おお時間の痕跡はぼくの正六面體の室内を雪のように激変せしめる。すべり落された貂の毛皮のなかに発生する光の寝台。　彼女の気絶は永遠の卵形をなしている。　水陸混同の美しい遊戯は間もなく終焉に近づくだろう。　乾燥した星が朝食の皿で轟々と音を立てているだろう。　海の要素等がやがて本棚のなかへ忍びこんでしまうだろう。　やがて三直線からなる海が、ぼくの掌のなかで疾駆するだろう。　彼女の総體は、賽の目のように、あるときは白に、あるときは紫に変化する。空の交接。　瞳のなかの蟹の声、戸棚のなかの虹。　彼女の腕の中間部は、存在しない。　彼女が、美神のように、浸蝕されるのはひとつの瞬間のみである。　彼女は熱風のなかの熱、鉄のなかの鉄。しかし灰のなかの鳥類である彼女の歌。　彼女の首府にひと

A Kiss for the Absolute

A woman of pure intuition, barging into my sitting room that's
been soaked with the spray from the waterfall inside my golden
nails. I don't ask whether or not a hunter has made a raid on the
twinkling diamond on her finger. Cinched horizontally and ver-
tically in a dress, her breasts are like a balance filled to the brim.
Her faint mustache speaks of a natural disaster in the Country of
Wax. She is moving back and forth, coming and going in a lipstick
lens that is burning up time. The secret of personal pronouns.
The sensation of time. O traces of time that drastically change
the interior of my six-sided room, the way snow would. A bed
of light born inside a slipped-off sable stole. Her swoon assumes
an eternal oval. The beautiful game where one mistakes water
for land will soon come to an end. A dry star will rumble around
on a breakfast plate. The ocean elements, et cetera, will soon slip
into the bookshelves. Soon, a sea made of three straight lines
will gallop across my palm. Like dots on dice her wholeness
alternates—sometimes white, sometimes purple. The sky's coitus.
The crab's voice inside a pupil, a rainbow inside an armoire. Noth-
ing of her arm's midsection exists. For just one moment, she's

でが流れる。　彼女の彎曲部はレヴィアタンである。　彼女の胴は、相違の原野で、水銀の墓標が姙娠する焰の手紙、それは雲のあいだのように陰毛のあいだにある白晝ひとつの白晝の水準器である。　彼女の暴風。　彼女の傳説。　彼女の営養。彼女の靴下。彼女の確証。彼女の卵巣。彼女の視覚。彼女の意味。彼女の犬歯。無数の実例の出現は空から落下する無垢の飾窓のなかで偶然の遊戯をして遊ぶ。コーンドビーフの虹色の火花。　チーズの鏡の公有権。　婦人帽の死。　パンのなかの希臘神殿の群れ。　霊魂の喧騒が死ぬとき、すべての物質は飽和した鞄を携えて旅行するだろうか誰がそれに答えることができよう。彼女の精液のなかの眞紅の星は不可溶性である。　風が彼女の緑色の衣服（それは古い奇蹟のようにぼくの記憶をよびおこす）を捕えたように、空間は緑色の花であった。　彼女の判断は時間のような痕跡をぼくの唇の上に残してゆく。　なぜそれが恋であったのか？　青い襟の支

like some eroded Goddess of Beauty. She's the heat in the hot wind or the iron in an iron. Even so, her song is the bird in the ashes. A starfish is drifting into her capital. Her curved parts are leviathan. Her torso is a wilderness of difference, a flaming missive in which a mercury headstone becomes gravid, it's the broad daylight's spirit level, the daylight that lies, as if between clouds, between the hairs in a bush. Her tempest. Her legend. Her nutrition. Her bobby socks. Her solid evidence. Her ovaries. Her visual sense. Her significance. Her eye teeth. In an innocent show window that descends from the sky, the sudden appearance of countless actual examples playing games of chance:

> Corned beef with iridescent sparkles. The
> public property rights of a mirror of cheese.
> The dying of a lady's hat. A teeming swarm
> of Grecian temples inside a loaf of bread.

When the clamoring of souls dies down, will all matter go traveling with a suitcase filled to the brim, who can answer that? Inside her semen are insoluble crimson stars. As the wind caught her green dress (it jarred my memory like an ancient marvel), space was a green bloom. Her judgment leaves time-like traces on my lips. Why was this love? When a Chinese scholar with a blue

那人が扉を叩いたとき、単純に無名の無知がぼくの指を引っぱった。 すべては氾濫していた。 すべては歌っていた。 無上の歓喜は未踏地の茶殻の上で夜光虫のように光っていた . . . . . .　(sans date)

collar knocked at the door, a simply nameless lack of knowledge pulled at my fingers. All was overflowing. Everything was singing. Supreme delight was glowing like noctiluca sea sparkle on the leftover tea leaves of an untrodden path . . .   (*sans date*)

白の上の千一夜

　午前二時雲の親子たちは長椅子の上に尻尾のある湖水を抱きながら白いテーブルの上の夜明けを待っている

　　　　　　　　　　　　　　　　　　　　　　太陽のレースの瞳の髪飾りから数千歩のところで

　　　　　　　　　　　　　　　　　　闇へと脱出する叫ぶけむりの引きちぎった挨拶は結晶に血液を象嵌する手術

透明な豹の子の光のように折りたたまれて切り抜かれペリカンの空に亡霊のように花束のように

　　　　　　　　　　　　　　　浮かぶものは水すましの墓標と花たちと雲たちの永遠のくちづけのくぎづけであった

果てしない夜は小犬の拙い輪廓の中にやっとのことでその

One Thousand and One Nights on White

At two a.m. two clouds on a bench, one a parent, one a child, embrace a lake with a tail while waiting for day to break on a white table.

Several thousand steps away from the headband around the sun's lacy pupil,

a hello torn from the crying smoke that escapes into the dark is an operation by which a blood inlay is embedded in a crystal.

Whirligig-beetle gravestones floated with eternal kisses that were frozen between flowers and clouds like apparitions, like nosegay bouquets

folded and cut out like the light of a transparent panther cub in a pelican sky.

Limitless night just manages to sketch the direction of the eyes inside the

視線を描いたぼろぼろの夜の天窓が孤独な噴水のように開らかれた匂いたかく開らかれた

　　　　　　　　　月光の下で牡牛の化石した屍体から咲き出た内臓が湖水の畔りで眠っていた傳説はいま生ま木のように清潔で現実の悲劇はいま鏡のすべてのふちから裂けそうであったそして窓は閉じられた千年後にふたたび開らいてみるために

　　　　　　　　　盲いた花の扉たちは雲型の蝶番いで彼女の愛読書をひらく

　　　　　　　　　岩の中の無数の階段を読む悲劇の中のヒロインの永遠のつぶやきはミシンの音のようにつづく

不眠の夜彼女の夢の無限の突起の中で三つの湖水のあくびは忘却の白い山をうつす

　　　　　　　　　飢えた大理石の食卓の上で裂けた影たちのダンス　マカブルに眼と毛皮が不器用に歌う時

inexpertly drawn outline of a puppy. Night's tattered skylight was opened like a lonely fountain, was fragrantly opened.

In the moonlight, the viscera that had blossomed from the fossilized corpse of a steer were asleep by the lake, the legend was then as clean as green wood and the real tragedy was now quite likely to be split off from each edge of a mirror, and the window was closed only to be opened again after a thousand years.

The doors of a sightless flower have cloud-shaped hinges that open her favorite book.

The eternal murmur of a tragic heroine who's reading the countless steps inside a rock continues nonstop like the sound of a sewing machine.

On a sleepless night, in the endless projection of her dream, three yawning lakes reflect the Mont Blanc of a mind going blank.

When eyes and fur sing gracelessly in a danse macabre of torn shadows on a table of starving marble,

不幸な姿見の一隅から風は朽ち果てた扉と一緒に歩きだす
だろう

　　　蝙蝠傘の故郷へ

　　　　　　　　　やがて影たちは巨大な眼蓋を閉じ
難破船のごとく眠る

from one corner of an unfortunate full-length mirror, the wind
will begin to walk with a door crumbling to dust

to the birth-
place of umbrellas.

Soon the shadows close their enormous eye-
lids and sleep like shipwrecked ships.

DOCUMENT D'OISEAUX
鳥たちの記録

　鯉の星座に入った天使は梅の蕊の鏡を覗いて初めて私を知った。私の頭髪に麦の花を飾って走って行った。心臓の美しい魚が春になると天使の衣裳を盗むのである。この実験は蕾がこぼれんばかりの私の指先きで行われる。硝子の中で波が近く唸る。それは私の爪の上の初雪と私の腋の下の瀑布との会話的本能から生じた最初の晩餐であった。既に私の睫毛が夕日の色に染まると私の天使は大果実店からほとんど無形となって立ち去るのである。私はこの天使の職業を否定する。そして私は人形を割るようにこの桃のような天使を切ってみる。彼は歓喜に満ちた天使であった。そこに一個の悼ましい緑色の貝が破裂する。私は危険な処女である。私を巧みに誘惑する薔薇も然し永遠に泳ぐ比目魚に過ぎない。私のうなじに昇る小石のような純黄色の太陽を見給えよ。

　これは純粋に処女の想像である。さて私の黄金の耳輪を通ってくるすべての鳥たちには羽毛を与える。すべての微風

DOCUMENT D'OISEAUX: DOCUMENTING BIRDS

The angel joining the Koi star cluster took a peek at the mirror of a plum blossom's pistil and discovered me for the very first time. It decorated my hair with wheat flowers and then fled. At the beginning of spring, the fish with a beautiful heart steals the angel's costume. This experiment is performed at the tips of my fingers—which are teeming with buds. Inside a pane of glass, waves go roaring by. The initial banquet grew out of a conversational instinct between the season's first snowfall onto my fingernails and the waterfalls under my underarms. My eyelashes are already tinted the color of the setting sun when my angel is seen exiting a supersized fruit market, and is becoming nearly unbodied. I deny this angel's occupation. I then cut this peachy angel the way I would divide a puppet. He was a joyful angel. Right there, one sad green shell explodes. I am a dangerous virgin. Even so, the rose that so expertly seduces me is nothing but an olive flounder eternally swimming. Look at the pure-yellow sun that rises like an eely pebble up the nape of my neck.

This is purely a virgin's imagination. Now feathers are being handed out to every bird that flies through my gold earrings. A

には星の飛ぶ衣服を与える。　私の奇蹟は鈴なりの天の金剛石を懐胎することであった。　天使の影が魚類の光りによって私に落ちる。　彼の微笑はまことに神業であった。　彼の音声には透明無比な蜘蛛の巣の無限の城砦の効果があった。然しもはや唇は朱色のまま化石する。　無名となった一個の猫族のような美天使よ。　私はもう一度水晶のような麦の穂の汝の霊魂を通過せんことを希う。　血液を送附する花崗岩に感謝する。　驟雨は紫陽花の急行列車とひとしく天使の刺客である。　樹液に満ちた虹に刺される処女は私である。　鷲の中心はついに天使の薔薇色の毛髪を慕う。　それは理想的な萬有引力である。　波頭に今年の春も菫が咲いたのはその怖るべき結果である。　すべての海岸は全能であり、松の幹もまた一人のアポロンを孕む。　その髄のなかの無罪の悪魔の写真を見給え。　それは金剛石よりも美しく光り輝く。　天使よ。　この松の樹皮の下の電光広告によって汝の未来を知るのか。ここへ手をさしのべた天使の青空の屍體よ。鳥は円満である。彼の母親も円満である。　受胎した私は明るい蠟燭を喜悦とともに海中に携えてゆく。　これは鳥類にとって害毒であるか。否、今はすべての害毒が死滅する季節。　美的な氷山も今は産期にある。　一匹の金魚すら要塞の壁の上に光る。　至上の

star's flight suit is given to every breeze. My miracle was to be pregnant with an enormous cluster of heavenly diamonds. By the light of a class of fish, the shadow of an angel once fell on me. His smile was truly a miracle. His voice had the effect of an infinite fortress, an incomparably transparent spider's web. His lips have by now fossilized yet remain vermillion. You beautiful angel, like an entire cat breed whose name can no longer be brought to mind. I so wish I could again pass through thy soul, the crystalline ears of wheat. I thank the granite with blood in its veins. The sudden rainfall is both a hydrangea's express train and at the same time the angel's assassin. The virgin stabbed by a sap-filled rainbow, that's me. The core of the eagle eventually longs for the angel's rose-colored hair. This is an ideal universal gravitation. The terrifying result is that this spring, violets are again blooming on the crests of waves. Every shore is omnipotent and the trunk of a Greek fir tree again conceives an Apollo. Look at the photograph of the innocent devil in its heartwood. It shines more brightly than any diamond. O Angel! Is thy future known from the neon advertisement under the bark of this evergreen? O sky-blue angelic cadaver who reached out here to offer a hand. The bird is harmonious. His mother is also harmonious. I who am pregnant go into the sea with lightheartedness and a bright candle. Is this harmful to birds? No, now is the season when all harms are extinguished. The aesthetic iceberg is also now in the

海岸でシガールが燃える。それが水族館の最近の現象であることは秘密である。空気は骨の無い美姫である。ストローの内部で彼女は聖母である。その喉の PIAZZA で白薔薇のような宝石を落した。あの白い世界は島でもなく鳥でもなかった。その唯一の記憶がぼくを鬼にするだろう。朝がくるとすべての天使は起床する。彼らはふたたび永遠不滅であるその乳房を露出する。朝風は彼らにとって再びすがすがしかったのである。

　私は桃を彫刻しつつある神を盗み見たために死ぬ。私は立派な乳房を口に含みながら空色の薔薇束を抱きながら死んでいる。それは妙齢の冒険である。それによって蠅と宝石とは驚かない。海も一個の新しい楽器にすぎないからである。春を告げる美音の獅子は朝顔と人間を区別することのできない、そしてコバルトの日傘をさした完全な天體であった。これは劇的光景であった。水平線上の劇場よ。そとには四季、愛の鳥たちが囀っている。膃肭臍が七絃琴になることは、沈黙せよ。影のない太陽は私の便乗するヨットである。甲板の上で純白な神馬が跳ねているのを見る。ミューズは唯今化粧中であると、鳥たちの記録を見給え。

calving season. Even the single goldfish atop the fortress wall is glistening. On the paramount seashore, a cigar is burning. That this is a recent phenomenon in the aquarium is a secret. The air is an exquisite boneless princess. She's Our Lady in the straw. Gemstones are dropped like white roses into the PIAZZA of her throat. That white world was neither an isle nor an ibis. This sole recollection will turn me into a demon. When morning comes, the angels all rise and climb out of bed. They once again expose their eternally immortal breasts. Once again the morning breeze was refreshing.

Because I stole a glance at a god sculpting a peach, I die. I am dead with a magnificent breast in my mouth, embracing a bouquet of sky-blue roses. It's a youthful adventure. Neither flies nor gemstones are surprised. Since the sea is nothing more than a new type of musical instrument. The lion trumpets the spring with his beautiful voice yet can't distinguish between the face of a morning glory and a human, still he was a perfect celestial body holding a cobalt-blue parasol. That was quite a spectacle. O the theatre on the horizon line. Outside, lovebirds are twittering during *The Four Seasons*. On the subject of furry harp seals turning into seven-stringed zithers, shut your trap. This unshaded sun is the yacht on which I get a free ride. Sacred pure-white horses can be seen leaping across the deck. At the moment, the Muse is having her makeup done, so check out the documentary on birds.

断片

—danse des impuissants de la création. Tristan Tzara

　肉體の紅玉_{ルビ}がぼくの死ななかった肉體に光った。　紅玉が三秒間の寒冷をおぼえた。　青春期のヴィーナスの完全な頸がぼくを慰める。　肉體の紅玉が彼女の指にある。灰色の紅玉がぼくの指にある。

　夜とその他のすべてのものとが燦爛たる秤器の上で均衡をたもつ。　ぼくは火星を見る。　夜はぼくの魂をつつむ。ぼくはヒヤシンスを見る。夜はヒヤシンスをつつむ。冷酷な倦怠がぼくを動かす。　少女の裸體の魂が葦のように切断されようとして震えている。　ぼくはすべてのものを立ち去る。

　空想の悪魔が彼女に憑いた。彼女は阿呆のようになりぼくに白い指を見せる。　言葉を知らないぼくの魂が白百合のように膨れてくる。どうして彼女が変態したのか。　放蕩者の乳房は新しい貝殻の内部のように女性的になる。　ぼくの眼ははじめてそれを見ることができる。　彼女のとる不可解な姿態。

Fragments

—danse des impuissants de la création. Tristan Tzara

Some body's red ruby glistened in my body that hadn't yet been rubbed out. That ruby had had a three-second chill. The impeccable neck of a girlish Venus cheers me. Some body's ruby is on her finger. On my finger is a gunmetal-gray Ruby.

Nightfall and all other things are maintaining their equilibrium on a dazzling scale. I stare at Mars. Late evening in-folds my soul. I gaze at a hyacinth. Nighttime envelopes the hyacinth. Brutal indifference moves me. The essence of that youngish Venus's undressed body is about to be severed like a reed and is trembling. I take my leave leaving all behind.

Imagination's devil has now possessed her. She plays the fool and shows me her white fingers. Not knowing the proper words, my spirit begins to expand like a white sword-lily. Why has she transformed like this? The breasts of the libertine become feminized like the mother-of-pearl inside a new shell. My eyes can see this for the very first time. By way of the cryptic pose she assumes.

どの花にも似ない混雑した笑い。 限りなく変化したがる花
簪。 ああ恐るべき類似!

彼女は寂しさのために啜り泣く。

極端な女性のようになって着物につつまれている。 ぼくは
簡単なアジサイになる。 彼女は未知の肖像画を携えてぼくの
芸術に変化をあたえようとした。 彼女は傷ついた妖艶な腕
をぼくの前にさしだす。 とうとう空想の悪魔がぼくを捉えた。
ぼくはブルックリンの鉄橋の写真のほうに彼女の注意を向け
ようとした。 突然彼女はアジサイになる。

もし肉體が死ぬならばぼくは彼女を愛さない。

まったく同じスタイルの微風が三日つづく。 彼女は海岸に
出て鳥類の卵に酷似した膝を珍らしそうに撫でまわしている。
彼女はほとんど肉體を失ってしまったようだ。 彼女は葡萄の
実が永遠に持続するなら悲しくなると告白した。 彼女はぼく
の前で大理石の彫像のように食事する。 生きた白百合にさ
まざまな言葉がふりそそぐのを少女は気附かずにいる。 無
数の神々が驚くときすでに夜明けである。

The disordered hilarity that doesn't look like any flower. The ornamental flower-hairpin that wants to continue changing endlessly. Oh, terrifying similarity!

She's sobbing from loneliness.

Becoming very feminine wrapped in a kimono. I become a simple hydrangea. Bringing with her an unfamiliar portrait she tried to alter my art. Holding out her impaired but still captivating arms. Imagination's demon finally caught me out. I tried to redirect her attention to that photographic image of an iron bridge in Brooklyn. Suddenly she's changing into a lacehead hydrangea.

If that body dies, I will no longer love her.

An exact Beaufort-3 breeze lasts for three days. She's out on the beach and curiously kneading her knees that are near-miss matches for two bird eggs. The better part of her body now seems beyond reach. She confessed she'll sink into melancholy if bunches of grapes go on and on for eons. She's lunching before me as if she's a marmoreal statue. The girl is unaware of all the divergent words falling on a lively white daylily. When countless gods and goddesses get startled, it is already dawning.

ÉTAMINES NARRATIVES

1

　銅錢と白薔薇とが協和音を構成するとつばさのある睡眠が
さけびだす。　そのなかには異常に青い草が繁茂する地方へ
跳ねやる虹のように強靭な弾條がある。　田舎は土龍のよう
に美しいがその寒さにおののく掌は正確なので顔を蔽うのに
充分な引力を提供する。　すべての音を発する物質と同じに
あの睡眠も意志に属していたのかしら？　そこから脳髄が月
のように細密な脳髄が見える。　寒冷な鏡面には無数の神様
が附着している。　この瞬間の噴水は花のごとく綺麗である。
あふれる無用物をもって花の意志をもって新建築術をもくろむ
葉巻色の喉をした建築師の二つの眼は義眼である。　そして
彼の姓名がしだいに無機物に変化しつつあるのを意識してい
る。　ひとすじの黄金の光線は小鳥の発声器を突きとおした
まう。　合理的なる午前七時よ。

ÉTAMINES NARRATIVES

1

When the copper and the snow-white rose compose a harmony, sleep with wings lets out a howl. Inside it, a spring as resilient as a rainbow bounces over to a plain thick with blades of extremely green grass. The countryside is as beautiful as a mole, but hands shivering in the cold are so precise they provide enough gravity to cover the face. Like all sound-emitting matter, was that sleep also part of the will's work? Over there, a brain can be seen, a mind as intricate as a moon. Countless gods adhere to the mirror's icy surface. At this very instant, a flowing fountain is every bit as beautiful as a flower. The artificial eyes of that architect with a cigar-colored throat who is scheming a new architectural technique—via a flood of useless things, via a flower's willpower. An awareness of his name gradually turning into an inorganic compound. A ray of golden light pierces the vocal cords of a bird. O rational seven a.m.

2

　薔薇の眼をひらく塔へ不安定な飛翔をする満月の胸部は青く傷ついた風を記憶する。　天国の薬品を服用してから簡単な景色を見ている一人の少女を親切にする。完全な詐僞師が疾走する。　彼は衝突する。　花環のような海に。　星の色彩の犬に。　比較し得ない二つの拾得物に。　それから未知の光線に。　ついに無限に切断しうる花瓣のなかで溺死し得ない。

3

　変化する詩集に頭を載せる少年を呼吸する。　一つのコップを呼吸する。　鳥の骨骼は黄金になろうとする。　光線は落下しない。　薔薇と彼女とは停止せる夜間に最初の瞬間へかえる。　果物は微笑しない。　果物は羅針盤のように詩を知悉している。　果物は花の中の雑音を忘却し衰弱した緑色の窓について哄笑する。

4

　強壮な鳥は海面の上空から明瞭にかれらの都市を透視し冷たい突起で会話する孤独の宝石のようにめまぐるしい魂に

2

On a choppy flight to a tower that causes the rose's eyes to open, the pectoral zone of the full moon recalls a wounded blue wind. Kindness is shown to a girl staring at a plain landscape after she's taken a dose of celestial medicine. A perfect con man rushes in. He collides with a wreath-like sea, a dog with the color palette of a star, a pair of found objects that can't be compared, then, with an unexplained ray of light. Finally, he tries to drown himself in an infinitely severable petal but altogether fails.

3

Inspires a boy whose head is on a book of verse that keeps changing. A glass is being inspired. The skeleton of a bird is trying to turn into gold. The ray of light doesn't fall. On a night that comes to a standstill, she and the rose return to the very first moment. Fruit doesn't smile. Fruit grasps poetry as well as a compass. Fruit forgets that noises come from inside dandelions and then loudly cracks up over an enfeebled green window.

4

From the air above the surface of the sea a robust bird peers through their city for a bird's-eye view, then turns its breast to a soul as bewildering as isolated gemstones talking alone on a chilly

胸部を向ける。　動力の処女性に背を向ける花瓣商人の水色のほくろを化粧する都市は言語に訴えるものを持たない。　一羽の鳥の形態においてクローカスの不完全な唇に接吻をあたえない。　制限された天使は小鳥の同情心を明るくしたのち急に新しい眼球を籤めかえる。

5

　無数の神々の脳髄にある光澤ある山水画を姿勢のいい魚の眼球に移動する。　みずから粉砕する指先きに生誕する言葉は昨日と今日とを知らない。　美味な涙が緑草のような頬を流れるとき精密な時計面の湖水を疾走する幼いアフロディテの迅速な歩行を見たまえ。　旋回競争における春の季節の発達を見たまえ。　これが非常にうるわしい錯誤なきバスケットである。

6

　鏡面の垂直な酔いが早朝の冷たい花を襲う。　乳の愛が街街の無口な硝子窓を通って離散する。　眩しい不均衡の前

pier. The city that's applying makeup to the watery-blue mole on the flower merchant, who is turning his back on the maidenhead of the motive power, is missing any means of appealing to language. Regarding the figure of a bird, the imperfect lips of a crocus don't get kissed. After brightening the little bird's compassion, a lesser angel now suddenly adopts a new set of oculi.

5

An illustrious mountain-stream painting that exists in the brains of countless gods is moved into the eyes of a fish with upstanding posture. Words born at the fingertips only to be crushed know nothing of yesterday or today. Watch the rapid pace of a youthful Aphrodite running full speed ahead across a precise clock-face lake, as tears flow over her scrumptious grass-green cheeks. O, see now how the evolution of a spring can be seen in the loop-de-loop of a daredevil airshow. This is a very graceful infallible basket.

6

The tipsiness of the vertical surface of a mirror clobbers an icy flower in the early hours of morning. A love of milk passes through the even-tempered glass windows facing the urban streets, then scatters. The farmhand who willingly removes his cap in front of a blinding imbalance will never accept any categorical

で随意に帽子を脱ぐ農夫はかれの無上命令を葉緑素のこぼ
れる土龍のほかからは獲らない。　二つの黄金の月光のなか
で挨拶する。　二つの星のように優しくどなる。　華やかな生
の証拠にはにかみ季節を知らない婚礼衣裳のように死ぬ。詩
に向って防禦しない二つの喉笛がある。

imperative unless it comes from a mole spilling its chlorophyll. Greeting one another inside a pair of gold moonbeams. They kindly call out in the manner of two stars. They become bashful in the face of evidence of a splendid life and eventually die like an all-season wedding dress. Two windpipes can't stand up to poetry.

地上の星

I

鳥、千の鳥たちは
眼を閉じ眼をひらく
鳥たちは
樹木のあいだにくるしむ。

眞紅の鳥と眞紅の星は闘い
ぼくの皮膚を傷つける
ぼくの声は裂けるだろう
ぼくは発狂する
ぼくは熟睡する。

鳥の卵に孵った蝶のように
ぼくは土の上に虹を書く
脈膊が星から聴こえるように
ぼくは恋人の胸に頬を埋める。

II

耳のなかの空の
ぼくは星の俘虜のように

Stars on Earth

I

Birds, a thousand birds
close their eyes and open their eyes
Birds
suffer between trees.

Scarlet birds assault scarlet stars
and injure my skin
My voice will soon snap
I go mad
I sleep soundly.

Like a butterfly hatched in a bird's egg
I draw a rainbow on the ground
In order to hear the pulsing of a star
I bury both cheeks in my lover's breasts.

II

Like the prisoner of a star
in the sky inside an ear

女の膝に
狂った星を埋めた。

忘れられた星
ぼくはそれを呼ぶことができない
或る晴れた日に
ぼくは女にそれをたずねるだろう
闇のなかから新しい星が
ぼくにそれを約束する。

美しい地球儀の子供のように
女は唇の鏡で
ぼくを　ぼくの唇の星を捕える
ぼくたちはすべてを失う
樹がすべてを失うように
星がすべてを失うように
歌がすべてを失うように。

ぼくは左手で詩を書いた
ぼくは雷のように女の上に落ちた。

手の無数の雪が
二人の孤独を
手の無数の噴水が

I buried a demented star
in the woman's lap.

A forgotten star
I cannot call out to it
One fine day
I will ask the woman about it
From the dark a new star
promises it to me.

Like the offspring of a lovely globe
the woman captures me   and the stars of my lips
through the mirror of her lips
We lose everything
as trees lose everything
as stars lose everything
as songs lose everything.

I scribbled verses with my left hand
Like a bolt from the blue, I fell on the woman.

The myriad snowfalls of hands
the solitude of two people
the myriad fountains of hands

二人の歓喜を
無限の野のなかで
頬の花束は
船出する。

III

鳥たちはぼくたちをくるしくした
星たちはぼくたちをくるしくした
光のコップたちは転がっていた
盲目の鳥たちは光の網をくぐる
無数の光る毛髪
それは牢獄に似た
白痴の手紙である。

白いフリジアの牢獄は
やがて発火するだろう
そして涙のように
消えるだろう。

IV

鳥たちは世界を暖めた
ぼくの下の女は眼を閉じている
ぼくの下の女は眼を閉じている
鳥たちはぼくたちに緑の牧場をもってくる。

the delight of two people
in an infinite field
a bouquet of cheeks
sets sail.

III

Birds made us suffer
Stars made us suffer
Lit drinking glasses were lying about
Sightless birds pass through a net of light
Myriad glistening hairs
This moronic letter
that resembles a prison.

The white freesia prison
will soon catch fire
And vanish
like tears.

IV

Birds warmed up this world
Beneath me the woman has her eyes shut
Beneath me the woman has her eyes shut
Birds bring us green pastures.

彼女の肥えた牡牛のような眼蓋は
こがね色に濡れている
レダのように　聖な白百合のように
彼女の股は空虚である
ぼくはそこに乞食が物を乞うのをさえ見た
あらゆる悪事が浮遊していた
ぼくは純白な円筒形を動かすことができる。

佛陀は死んだ。

V

闇のように青空は刻々に近づく
ぼくは彼女の眞珠をひとつひとつ離してゆく
ぼくたちは飛行機のように興奮し
魚のように悲しむ
ぼくたちは地上のひとつの星のように
ひとつである
ぼくの精液は白い鳩のように羽搏く
ぼくは西藏の寺のように古い詩を書く
そしてそれを八つ裂きにする
ぼくは詩を書く
ぼくは詩を書く
そしてそれを八つ裂きにする

Her eyelids like those of a fatted calf
are the color of gold
Like Leda   like a holy white lily
her torso-fork is empty
I even spotted a beggar begging there
All sorts of malices were floating about
I can even move the pure white cylindrical form.

The Buddha is dead.

V

Like the darkness each instant brings the blue sky nearer
One by one I take off her pearls
We get turned on like airplanes
and grow sad like fish
Like one star on earth
we are one
My gametes flutter like a dole of doves
I write a verse as old as a Tibetan temple
Then tear it to pieces
I write a verse
I write a word temple
Then tear it to pieces

それは赤いバラのように匂った
それはガソリンのように匂った。

氷のように曇った彼女の頬が見える
花のように曇った彼女の陰部が見える
そして鳥たちは永遠に
風のなかに住むだろう
狂った岩石のように。

盲目の鳥たちは光の網を潜る。

It smelled of red roses
It smelled of gasoline.

Her cheek seen fogged like ice
Her sex seen misted like flowers
And birds will go on forever
living in the wind
like erratic rocks.

Sightless birds pass through a net of light.

実験室における太陽氏への公開状

I

　《天使の種子の眼に会話する新水晶は私の最初のけむりである。　鏡と鏡とのあいだの畑よ。　ヴァロンの谷よ、この霊感をうけた螢の天然色の原理が際限のない夏の女神であるのを女神自身は知らない。　廻廊の急激な王子の死は不滅、物質もまた不滅である。　瞬間の祭礼・永遠の祭礼の妖精のDENTELLE は鳶のごとく私の胸中を舞う。　これが高度な鯖の頭蓋の文明を意味したか否か、おお巨大な純黄色の乳房のマニキュールに聴くがよい。　彼女は彼女が孤独な愛すべき妖怪屋敷であることを歌う。　彼女もまた絶対であることに私は動揺する松柏類のアポロンとともに乾盃する。　彼女は出現である。　彼女はガラス體のなかの稲妻　扇型の音の曇らない蜘蛛の巣　現象の歓呼　愛の海　彼女は出現である。彼女は自然の寵児・柳・硫酸・風に吹き寄せられた雪、少女よ、この無愛想な群れに驚きたまうな。　彼女は妖精型である。彼女は未知の怪奇なけむりを吐く最新の結晶體、死後の思春

Open Letters to Mr. Sun in the Laboratory

I

"The new crystal that converses with an angel's seedlike eyes is my first smoke. O cultivated field between two mirrors. O valley in Vallon, the goddess of endless summer doesn't know that she herself is the inspiring principle behind the firefly's natural color. The sudden death of a prince in a hall is an immortal thing, what the matter is is also immortal. The lace DENTELLE of the fairy of the Forever Festival, the festival of this moment, dances in my heart like a kite. Whether this indicated the civilized state of a sophisticated mackerel braincase or not, oh, go listen to the French *manucure* with huge pure-yellow breasts. She sings the fact that she is a lovely lonely haunted mansion. I myself raise a glass with a stirred-up cone-bearing Apollo to toast the fact that she too is an absolute. She is appearing. She is a lightning bolt in the vitreous humor   a fan-shaped spider web of sound that doesn't get misted over   phenomenal cheering   a sea of love   she is appearing. She is a beloved child of nature, a willow, oil of vitriol, drifting snow blown by the wind, O dear girl, don't be surprised by this discourteous circle. She is a fairy type. She is the latest crystal emitting a mysterious and unknown smoke, a

期である。　これらの私の力説の天然色を判じたまえ。明日
もまた彼女である。明日の建造物のほんのりとした薄紅色の
窓から私は私の食物を攝取するとき黄金色の若い自転車乗
りがその若い妻に向かって微笑しているのを見た。　その若
い妻の額に絶対心理の図絵があることを熱望した。　あらゆ
る形態の小鳥たちが彼の頭上を円舞した。スイートピーの形
の小鳥たちが幸か不幸か路上に墜落した。彼の妻はそれを
拾うことを知っていた。　これは愛情のみであった。これは必
然の脅威、花束のヒッポドローム、表情が　見たまえ　あの雲
の燭光この雲の燭光である。　葦は絶対的に繁茂するイリュミ
ナシオンである。　苛酷の論理のマニキュール天使の眩惑する
イロニー・私はきみにすこしも似ていない。　天国の一種であ
る私の瞳の座席で私は水色の馬に面会する。　秘密は歌う歌
を歌う。　秘密は自然の真理である。いやむしろ要因である。
人間は荘厳な人間である。　人間は美しい人間である。汝の
財宝を知れ。ある朝マニキュールは朝顔の毛髪、水の爪を想
像した。　彼女は純粋真紅な鶏と同年である。白熊の爪が彼
女を驚かすための奇術であったのは彼女の天恵である。　ロ
ゴスは彼女の唯一の顔面。　波頭の装飾　星の文字は彼女
の偶然の記号にすぎない。　彼女は適応の驚異すべき女性

posthumous pubescence. Judge the natural color of all my emphases. Tomorrow is also her. From a pale, faintly pink window of a building built tomorrow, while I was consuming my nutrients, I saw a gold-colored young bicycle rider smiling at that young wife. Wishing that on that young wife's brow there might be a depiction of an absolute state of mind. Little birdies of every shape danced, circling above his head. For better or for worse, the little birdies shaped like sweet peas collided with the street. His wife knew about picking those up. That was love alone. This is an inevitable threat, the bouquet's hippodrome racecourse, the look on the face that says   Look   that cloud's candlelight, this cloud's candlelight. *Les Illuminations* is a reed that is sure to flourish. The *manucure* of cruel logic, the angel's enchanting irony: I don't look like you at all. On the seat of my eyes, which is a kind of heaven, I meet a watery-blue horse. A secret sings a singing song. The secret is nature's truth. Or rather, it's a factor. Humans are sublime human beings. Humans are lovely human beings. Know thy treasure. One morning, the *manucure* imagined the hair of a morning glory and claws of water. She's the same age as a pure-vermillion chicken. That the claws of a polar bear were a sleight-of-hand trick to surprise her is her blessing from heaven. Logos is her sole façade. The alphabetic letters of a star, the ornamental white horses along the tops of waves, are merely her accidental signs. Is she a female god whose adaptability is amazing? ÉVEN-

神？ ÉVENTAIL D'INTELLIGENCE　彼女が海神の上流の襟飾りを見ることが可能であったのは彼女の思想、彼女の雲間の思想、彼女の辯護は私の思想、驚くべき虹の一致＊＊＊》

　　太陽氏よ、ぼくの稲妻入りの壁面が夢に描かれたのだと看破したのは譬えばきみの優美な水泳術に値いするだろうか。きみの純粋な楕円形の頭脳は星のために汚されない。　星のように美しい。　そんなに笑い給うな。　錦の蝶々がぼくの眼蓋の下の空間を縮れた幼いテレマックのように数限りなく通過する。　テレマックの固有名詞を全く知らない猫柳の製造家、ときに黄金の色彩を放つ彼の驚愕も塗漆師の小羊が彼女の純白な円筒の口を発見したことにくらべれば極小の蜘蛛の子ほどでもない。　純白　はじめて知ったこのコトバは形容詞であるか、動詞であるか、名詞であるか、固有名詞であるか、接続詞であるか？　たとえばきみの指輪はきみの天使の指に嵌まるだろうか？　この論理はただしい。　しかし彼らが純白の精神に対して無関心であるのはいかにも滑稽である。　白熊の音楽にさえ無関心ではないか。風の想像。雷鳴の意識。それはきみの発明。そして純白もまたきみの発明であるか。しかし純白は鳴く。　私はむしろやつあたりである。　きみはそれを理解するだろう。　きみは私のように氷の王冠を食うだろう。

TAIL D'INTELLIGENCE: her way of thinking, her cloud-clearing way of thinking, was the reason she could see the up-streaming necktie of the sea god, her defense is my way of thinking, an astounding concurrence of rainbows * * * "

Mr. Sun, is it worth your graceful swimming skills, for example, to have realized that my lightning-bolt walls were painted in a dream? Your pure egg-shaped brain will not be tainted by stars. As beautiful as stars. Don't crack up laughing like that. Damask butterflies countlessly pass by in the space beneath my eyelids, like a shrunken young *Télémaque*. The amazement of the pussy-willow-propagator who doesn't even know the proper noun *Té-lémaque*, and who sometimes emits his own golden rays, is not even an itsy-bitsy-spider when compared with the fact that the lacquer-master's lamb discovered her mouth on a snow-white cylinder. Snow-white—is this word, which I learned for the first time, an adjective, verb, noun, proper noun, or a conjunction? For example, can your ring fit the finger of an angel? This logic is correct. It is indeed comical that they are indifferent to the spirit of snow-white. Indifferent even to the music of polar bears. And the mind of the wind. And the awareness of thunder. That is your invention. Is snow-white also your invention? But snow-white cries. I'd rather vent my anger. You will understand that. Like me, you will eat a crown of ice.

不安家よ。　彼らの袖はどこまで長いか太平洋に届くか北極まで届かないかと不安になるきみの脳髄は坐骨神経痛であるかそうでもないか。　ぼくは著述する。　湖水のなかで水晶のごとく先天的に著述する。　ぼくはむしろ月界を旅行するヒトデに同情をもつ。　それはやや以前からであった。朱色の喉は予言されていたのであった。　これは色彩家以外に誰をも困らせない。　彼らは種々な幾億の糸杉を夢みたのだが、記憶として黄金の液体が一滴舞い上ったばかりであった。　これはまだ誰にも話さなかったお伽ばなしの結末のひとつであるが私ははじめて純白に向かって公開する。　純白は鳴く。　彼らはありとあらゆる動物が混合されたリボンにすら平気である。　彼らはそれを記念物と思わず純粋装飾物と思う。　それは彼らの唯一の完全である。　思考することのできぬ色彩は彼らを刺戟しない。　彼らの恐怖心は怖れをなしている。　彼女の色彩よ。　彼女たちは幽霊のように新しい女たちだ。　敢ていえば彼女たちはサラダ菜のような肩をしている。部分であるが完成したものである。　そこには森羅萬象を具有した港がある。　平凡な男はこんな同時性的外観を蜃気楼と誤認しそれをかなりの光栄と思うだろう。眉が青磁色の水平線であった女優がすべての感覚から自由になりえたということはさもありそうなことだ。　最近、野芹の室内からひとつの展望が許された。　新アルプスとその不思議な氷河、それが決して一致点を見いださないという理由で実験室におけるきみの注意を

O nervous Nellie. Is your brain that worries about the length of their sleeves, whether they'll reach the Pacific Ocean, or whether they'll reach the North Pole, suffering from sciatica or not? I write. As innately as crystals in lake water. I sympathize with the starfish that travels within the lunar realm. That was a little while ago. A red throat was foretold. This wouldn't trouble anyone but colorists. Although they had dreamed of a billion kinds of cypresses, just now the memory of one drop of gold liquid rose up. This is one conclusion to a fairy tale that I've never told anyone, but I am exposing it to the public for the first time for snow-white. Snow-white cries. They are fine with ribbons mixed with all kinds of animals. They do not see them as mementos but as pure decoration. That is their sole perfection. A color that isn't able to think does not stimulate them. Their fear is frightful. O her hue. They are new specter-like women. They have, so to speak, lettuce-like shoulders. It is a portion but perfect. It is the harbor that holds everything under the sun. Ordinary men would mistake such a contemporary outlook as mirage and be honored by it. It's quite likely that the actress whose eyebrows were a celadon-green horizon was emancipated from all the senses. One outlook was recently permitted from the inside of a wild-parsley room. The novel alpine mountain and its strange glacier and why one can never find the point of confluence is why I called your attention to the laboratory. It's sacrile-

喚起した。　太陽氏の顔を想像することは冒瀆である。　もしくは極端な文明人であり（不明）彼の水銀が彼の唾液であるか否かということが問題である。　なぜなら氏の顔はもはや手のごとくであり翼のごとくであり眞珠のごとくでありタングステンのごとくでありそのすべてでもなくそのすべてが可能である歓楽を具有するからである。　太陽氏は月光のこぼれる河畔を散歩するだろう。　彼の純紅色のバッグ——このなかに実は水曜日と金曜日とが金の鷲と霊感と一緒に入っている——を運びながら。　尤もこういう光景には彼らはあまり親密ではないであろう。　予期したことでもなく予期しなかったことでもない現象である。　しかしその必然と当然と判然とを知るのはきみだけである。　朝顔の方法論はかならずしも円形劇場を必要としないかならずしも初雪を必要としないかならずしもピレネー……わが愛する太陽氏よ。　きみの全能があのぎらぎらと光る紫色の斑点に移動することは美麗な時代精神であるだろうか。太陽氏よ　きみは同姓同名の天體の運行をおそらく想像できるだろう。　あの不完全な象徴!　しかしその優雅な運行はきみのソプラノにすら値いするだろうか。　もし彼らが三半規管を疑わないと假定したまえ。　きみの声こそ透明な卵形の酸素儀礼であるか装置であるか。　とくにきみの産ぶ声を形容する専門家は残念ながら皆無である。　だからそれについては断念することが唯一の方法である。　ここには無思想というもっとも完全な體系が燈心草の内部として秘密のように自然

gious to imagine the face of Mr. Sun. The question is whether he is extremely civilized (unknown), and whether or not his quicksilver is his saliva. Because the face of Mr. Sun is like a hand like a wing like a pearl like tungsten and it possesses the pleasure that makes all of that possible even though it is not all of that. Mr. Sun will stroll along a riverbank on which moonlight trickles. Carrying his pure-crimson bag—inside it is actually Wednesday, Friday, a golden eagle and inspiration all together. Of course, they are not familiar with a view like this. That is a phenomenon that is neither expected nor unexpected. But only you know its necessity, inevitability, and clarity. The strategy of a morning glory does not necessarily need an amphitheater, nor does it necessarily need a first snow, nor does it necessarily need the Pyrenees … my beloved Mr. Sun. Is the fact that your omnipotence moves toward that glaring purple spot a gorgeous zeitgeist? Mr. Sun, you can probably imagine the movement of the celestial body that has your same name. That imperfect symbol! But is that graceful movement even worthy of your soprano? Assume that others don't doubt the ear's three semi-circular canals. Is your voice that very same transparent, ovoid oxygen ritual, or a device? More to the point, there is no longer any expert who could now describe your birth cry. Thus, the only thing to do is to give up. This is related to the fact that the most perfect system, which is called unthinking, exists, like secrets, like nature, inside lantern plants.

のように存在していることが関連している。 無思想の原型が無生物金剛石にまで溯ることはもしそれが新型の鰻でなければ証明不可能であろうか。「無想像」の区域を長大な美神が専横の形態で潜りつつある現場はただ想定することも不可能である。 眼窩の虚無は盲目を意味するだろうか。その内部をヴィーナスとしての白金線が通過することは不可解で馬鹿げているだろうか。 遠近官能を欠除した先験的視覚が鰻の形態を日々完全に誘導していることはほぼ感じられた。 彼が球根植物に変化するという民間科学説は彼の稲妻のユーモアをあらわすものでなくて何であろう。 胎生学と結晶学とがきみのコバルトの冷却室で心臓が抱擁礼をしたことを祝福する。 いまや紺碧の岩間でシネマが語る時刻である。 似而非全能の岩魚が微笑む。 全裸體の緋鯉よ。 太陽氏に感謝せよ。 あるいはきみはきみのスタイルで悪態のかぎりをつくしてもきみは愛せらるべきである。 無思想は卵生支那人の発明だけではなく思考する白鶴の破壊者dadaは理想的天蓋の眞空劇場の愛人たちであった。 無思想について無愛想がある。 これにもおなじく太陽氏の創造力が反応する。 寒帯動物が雲に包まれた薔薇を恋する風景論がたんに彼らの無愛想であるのは不思議である。 波だつ貝殻の内部に人間の声が柔順である。 彼の旗は♥である。 あらゆる言語に反対

Unless it's a new type of eel, wouldn't it be impossible to prove that the original model for un-thinking can be traced back to inanimate diamonds?   It is also impossible to imagine a scene where a gigantic goddess of beauty is about to brazenly dive into the realm of "the un-imagined." Does the eye socket's emptiness always mean blindness?   Is it impossible and silly to make a platinum inoculation-loop pass like Venus through the eye socket? It's almost as if the transcendental vision of eyesight, lacking any sense of perspective, was, day by day, precisely dictating the shape of the eel.   What's the popular-science theory that the sun transfigures into a plant bulb if not to demonstrate the humor of his lightning?   Embryology and crystallography bless the fact that hearts embraced and said "Hi" in your cobalt cooling room.   Now is the hour when cinema will be discussed among deep-blue stones. A phony omnipotent *iwana* fish smiles.   O red carp with a stark-naked body. Thank Mr. Sun.   Even if in your own style you use the most abusive language possible, you should be adored.   The un-thinking is not just the invention of the cosmic-egg-born Chinese, but dada, the destroyer of thinking white cranes, lovers in airless theatres under idealized canopies. After un-thinking, there's coldness. To this, too, Mr. Sun's creativity responds. It's a queer landscape theory that says the arctic animals' love of roses wrapped in cloud covers is merely due to their coldness. A human voice is obedient inside a billowy shell. His banner is a ♥. Because

の二つの方向なぜなら幻は抽象を創造し彼らの完全な形體のなかで不思議の国を展開する。 そこに貝殻たちはまったく人間の言葉を形成する。 きみの♥は鏡であるか？ 氷山に等しい猫は嗅覚の暦を創造するだろうと冥想家は考える。 ここでは彼の唾液は旗である。 螢に認識された要素、月蝕の紙がクレオパトラに似ない美女を透かす。彼女の櫻色の眼球は連想を拒絶した。 ひとびとはもはや彼女の思想を知覚しない。 海波か電波か区別のつかぬ程度に彼女を見知らない。無知の円舞はこの地球を装飾する。しかし装飾は意識として第一位の尊敬である信念の天恵がややもすれば不平等であった人間たちも、意識の地下ではたとえば装飾学についてもいちじるしくその権威が転倒せられ、人は価値そのものの存在をも容易に忘却せんとする。 そして鯛の眼窩の現行犯とマッタホルンの現行犯とを区別することを漸次抛棄しはじめるや否や彼は単に湖水上の現行犯となる。 たとえば倒さ富士の犯人は誰れ？ 人は朝の挨拶よりももっと簡単にそれを口にすることができたであろう。 きみの実験室ではすべてが犯されていない。 豚の傍の眞珠は客観的に眞実である。それ

illusions create abstractions, which in their perfected forms unfold into a wonderland, there are two opposing directions in every language. There, shells form a completely human language. Is your ♥ a mirror? A meditator thinks that a cat matched by an icecap would create a calendar of olfactory senses. Here, his saliva is a banner. The element noted by some fireflies—a slip of paper viewed through the light around a lunar eclipse reveals a beautiful woman who does not look like Cleopatra. Her cherry-blossom-colored oculi refuse associations. People no longer perceive her thinking. They don't know her well enough to tell an ocean wave from a radio wave. Backward waltzes decorate this earth. However, even among humans, who have been some-what unequally blessed by belief—in which decoration as a form of consciousness is given the highest level of respect—in the underground of consciousness, the authority in the field of decorative studies, for example, has been significantly overturned and people try to forget the existence of value itself. As soon as one gradually starts to give up distinguishing between the caught red-handed sea-bream-eye-socket crime and the red-handed Matterhorn crime, he himself is simply caught red-handed on a lake. Who, for example, is the perpetrator of the upside-down reflection of Mount Fuji on the lake? A human could have uttered that more easily than a "Good-morning" greeting. Not everything has been perpetrated in your laboratory. "Pearls cast before swine"

は未制定な審美的定理のひとつである。 認識は無数以上であった。 矩形の判断は超動物的白熊によってある睡蓮に適用されたといっても不平をこぼすにはあたらない。 円虫類は幸いなるかなという憐憫の情も単なる抒情的反語にすぎないのである。 現実に対する趣味には黒人の睡眠病がより多く満足をあたえるであろう。論理は鏡の三叉路においてすら優雅である。 彼女の任意の大洋へ流れよ。 彼女こそは仙女である。 美しい球體の眞珠は彼女の論理をもつ。

桔梗は彼女の多少激烈な論理で裂けた。 四季の花、秋の七草、その感性なき発生はその容姿の特徴は太陽氏の実験の模倣とも見える。 雲型定規の神出鬼没の運用、それは単なる一例にすぎない。 運命は有限な一思想的存在であるから爆沈は水晶の指なのである。 鬼火の指輪よ。 きみの指はなんと愛に燃える!

無視、それは方法であるか。 それは彼女の胸の反対のほうで風を孕む帆船の無限の否定であるか。 おおぼくを厭悪したまえ。 対象の論理が撃破されたのはすでに紀元前であったと信じられる現在の文明の限界がある。 イリュミネーションの食物が象徴する全爬行の世界、金剛石の靴が腐敗する世界、蘭が錆びた朝、これは観念の過失にすぎないのだろうか。

is a form of objective truth. That's one of those unestablished aesthetic theorems. Perception used to be greater than infinity. Even if an ultra-animal polar bear misjudged a water lily as a rectangle, it's not worth complaining about. "Blessed are" the roundworms although such compassion is nothing but mere lyrical irony. Tsetse-fly induced sleeping sickness gives more satisfaction to the taste of daily reality. Logic is elegant even in a mirror's three-way street. Drift toward her willing ocean. She herself is a nymph. The pearl of a beautiful orb embodies her logic.

Her rather violent logic ripped off a blue balloon flower. Flowers of four seasons, seven fall flowers, that senseless genesis, the characteristics of its appearance seem to be an imitation of the Mr. Sun experiment. The elusive use of a set of French curves is but one example. Because fate is only one finite ideological state, the crystal's fingers blow up and sink. O will-o'-the-wisp ring. How your fingers burn with love!

Look the other way, is that the approach? Is it the infinite disowning of a sailboat pregnant with wind at the opposite end from her breasts. Fine, so sue me. There is a limitation on modern civilization, which is being able to believe that the logic of being an object had already been crushed back in BCE. The wholly creepy-crawly world, symbolized by the nourishment of illumination, a world in which diamond slippers rot, mornings

人は空中に向かって融ける科学的適用の氷に胸が騒ぐが、あなたの乳房のなかの氷山のそして笑くぼについてはあなたは美しい眼を瞑ってしまっていた。　ある憂欝な眼またはあまりに単純な眼はそれが心理現象のひとつにすぎないと断言することによってしきりに可笑しがろうとする。

II

　太陽氏よ、君のなかの燃焼物質を分析してみたまえ。　微細な蟹と高尚な鶴の心臓、危険信号燈……　君の声はもう変わっている。　君は毎日のように完全な変貌をとげつつある。君は君の天使を絶えず放射しつつ哄笑を霊感する。　典型物とは何か？　およそこのことに就て最も無知な人間は君なのである。　六つの花葵はひとつ宛つ天使を抱きながら紫であった。　ひとつの花葵は火力電気であった。　ひとつの花葵は人工営養であった。　ひとつの花葵は北極探検であった。ひとつの花葵は聖母受胎であった。　ひとつの花葵は石灰質であった。　このように空虚のなかの精は夢のガラスのなかで転々とする（君とぼくとの間に如何なる関係があるのか？）これほど滑稽な問題があるだろうか？　永遠の髭が生えた水硝子のような太陽氏よ、天使よりも愛らしい太陽氏よ、ルイ・アラゴン

when orchids rusted, could this be nothing but a failure of ideas. As human beings are stirred up by scientifically produced ice melting up toward the sky, you closed your beautiful eyes to icebergs inside your own chest and to dimpled cheeks. Certain melancholic eyes or oversimplified eyes try to grin and bear it by asserting that it's nothing but a single psychological phenomenon.

II

O Mr. Sun, you must analyze the flammable matter at your core. Lousy microcosmic crabs, the hearts of high-minded cranes, flashing hazard lights . . . Your voice has already changed. Daily you undergo a complete transformation. While endlessly emanating your heavenly angels, you inspire a cloudburst of laughter. What is a type of ur-thing? On this subject, you are by far the most unlettered person. Six hollyhocks turn purple while embracing angels one by one. One hollyhock acted as a thermoelectric generator. One hollyhock was bottle-fed. One hollyhock was on an Arctic expedition. One hollyhock was the Immaculate Conception. One hollyhock was limestone-like. Like this, the spirit in the void rolls around in the glass of a dream. (What is the nature of the relationship between you and me?) Is there a problem as comical as this one? Mr. Sun, who is like soluble glass with an unending five-o'clock shadow, Mr. Sun, who is lovelier

ではないが、君の波長とぼくの波長とを計算する科学者は誰れだ。 ぼくの脳髄は宏壮なスケート場のように青くひらめいている。これは「花葵なの？」と聞くのは不思議である。 ぼくが夢みるとき一層不思議である。 虚無のなかに何があるか？ 何ものも無い、唯だ、太陽氏よ、君の絢爛たる肉體のほかには。 むしろ君は無数の典型の創始者である。 典型よ、消失せよあるいは誕生せよ。 君は典型の花束に埋れている。 君は典型のみである。 雷鳴よ、君は典型である!

　ぼくは絶対紙にしたためている。 君は昨日リトマス紙の妖怪をぼくに郵送した。 あのナイアガラ瀑布の音のする、そしてあの微妙な激戦の見える、そのなかのひとつの爆発が千倍の愛撫に化した紙、そこに君は何らの眺望をも許さなかったのは後天的装置であったろうか？　無風景の世界に、君は君の澄明な胸の海のなかに青い夢を見る。君はその青い潮を如何にして天に上げようかと考えているのか？　ぼくが君を夢みるとき君もぼくを夢みる。 これは相似形體では説明がつかなかった。 なぜならこれら二つの夢は衝突したから。 それは二つの美しい鳩にくらべることが出来るだろうか？ 実はまったく新しいひとつの感情の生誕であった。 恋愛と見違えるほどに新しいひとつの感情。 ぼくはニッケルのパラソルが魚の眼球を吸う春を目撃した。 魚の眼は君の先天性を疑うほどである。 暗澹とした鏡の室内で先天性が無限に旋回する。

than an angel, if it's not Louis Aragon, who is the scientist who takes the measure of your wavelength and mine? My brain glows blue like a magnificent skating rink. It's odd to pose the question, "Is this a hollyhock?" When I'm dreaming, it grows stranger still. What is inside nothingness? Nothing, Mr. Sun, other than your gorgeous body. Rather, you are the originator of countless archetypes. O ur-type, disappear or be born. You are buried in a bouquet of archetypes. You are only an archetype. Thunderclap, you are an archetype!

I am unequivocally writing this on a sheet of paper. Yesterday you mailed me a little devil in the form of a strip of litmus paper. Right here the sound of those Niagara Falls is overheard, and in those subtly turbulent battles that are seen on paper, one explosion turns into a thousand-fold caress: is the non-innate nature of the equipment the reason you didn't allow any panoramic views. In the world of the non-scenic landscape, in the sea of your clarified chest, you are dreaming a blue dream. How do you plan to raise that blue tide into the sky? When I am dreaming about you, you are dreaming me up. The similar shapes didn't explain it. Because the two dreams collided, one with the other. Can they be compared to two beautiful doves? It was truly the onset of a novel feeling. A new feeling that could be mistaken for love. I witnessed a spring where a nickel-plated parasol was sucking up to a fisheye. The fisheye is casting doubt on your innate properties. In a dark

太陽氏よ、君は君の性質を持っているのか否かが怪しい。君は君の絹の愛馬の上で紫水晶の天狗に遭遇する。君は偶然に恵まれた不思議国の創造者。　君は君の甲板に出た瞬間の星月夜に最新プラトニシァンの波しぶきをかけられた。もはや寓意の時間は去っている。　君のガラスの心臓は君のためにのみ鼓動する。　凡ての郵便物は御覧独特の意味をもつようになった。　水色の樹液が樹々から彼らの影を奪った。その時君の手も水色に澄んでいた。　そして君もまたいそがしく書簡紙の上にペンを走らせる。君は未来の影のためにダイヤの波濤のように進化する。　おおぼくを魅惑するのはこのような運動の外には無かった。深海の雪達磨は声を発する。その腋からの光線で雛鳥が育つ。　この時電話がかかってきた。紫の波からである。彼女の言語は数億世紀からの歴史を震動している。　それが蝶の眼鏡を通して見える。　そしてこれが現実、現実の六角柱である。　純白の火は君の足跡に燃える。　純白の火は舞う。　彼女の片足をあげる。　純白の魔杖を振る。　まあ純白の噴火を見給え。　ついに純白の火山灰のなかで純白の猿が眠っていた。　発狂した雪花石膏のように繊細な星がゆらゆら君に面会する。　君がそれを再認するスタイルは典雅であった。　それが世界史のどの世紀に属し

room mirror, innateness circles endlessly. O Mr. Sun, it's doubtful whether you have your own temperament. On your favorite silk horse, you encounter an amethyst *Tengu* goblin. You are the creator of a wonderland favored by chance. The moment you climbed up on the ship's tossed deck, the starry night splashed you with latest Platonist's sea spray. The time for allegories has already passed. Your glass heart beats only for you. Look, every piece of mail came to have a unique meaning. Watery-blue sap robbed trees of their shade. At that moment, your hands were also transparent in the watery-blue. And you, too, kept busy letting a pen run on stationery. For the shade of the future, you evolve like a surge of diamond-shaped waves. Oh, outside such movement there was nothing to dazzle me. From deep in the sea, a snowman speaks. Light rays from under its arms raise little birdies. At this moment, a phone rang. From a purple wave. Her language convulses the history of several hundred million centuries. That is seen through a butterfly's spectacles. This is reality, the six-sided pillar of reality. Snow-white fire burns in your footsteps. Snow-white fire dances about. Lifts her foot. Waves a snow-white magic wand. Just look at the snow-white volcanic eruption. A white snow monkey was finally asleep on snow-white volcanic ash. Like crazed alabaster, a flimsy star wobbles in to meet you. The manner with which you recognized it was elegant. It's impossible to speculate as to which century in

ているかを思想することは出来ない。　君は君の眼を疑わない。　旋風が見舞う。　笑いの霊感の銅像がある。　倒された葦とともに柔軟な女神の素足が春の遺跡のように横たわっている。　春の亡霊は蛋白質の河底深く騒動を起す。　暴風の妙技は女神の手袋を望遠鏡とすり換える。　空の黒子が静かに全能の記憶をたどって太陽氏の美しい上気した頬に宿る。　水準器のなかの天女は逆さになって化粧している。　太陽氏の悲劇は不可能であった。　君は羽を慄わしたまま蚊のように荘厳になる。君は俳優ではない。　再認者である。　君は誤謬のない光線の THE PURE COMEDY に愛人の絹帽子となって転ろげ落ちる。　それは君のひとつの出現にすぎない。　君は謎ではなかった。　愛人のひらひらする白い眩しいスカートと打ち寄せる黒い波とのあいだのメタフィジシァンのように見える。軽卒な思想者よ。　君は無意味ではない。　被発見者になったと思うや否や THE END OF THE FIRST PART である。これは無意味ではない。　意味ではない。　永遠に終結しないものは一體何かと怪しむだろう。　氷のシネマに氷の観客、ぼくは君の温度のために凍死せんばかりになる時ぼくも氷になろうと決断する。　そして僕に青春が訪れた時初めて融解して幽邃の岩間を血液のように循環するだろうと占断する。　この時初めて氷の扉を黄金の天使である虹色の羊歯が飛行機の

world history it belongs. You don't doubt your eyes. A dust devil shows up. There's a bronze statue that inspires laughter. Together with beaten-down reeds, the flexible bare feet of a goddess lie like the ruins of spring. The ghost of spring creates a disturbance deep in the albuminous riverbed. With exquisite skill, a storm makes a switcheroo: the goddess's gloves for a spyglass. A sky's mole quietly retraces an omnipotent memory then moves in on the beautiful blushing cheek of Mr. Sun. An upside-down heavenly nymph inside a spirit level is making up her face. Mr. Sun's tragedy is impossible. Wings fluttering, you become an august mosquito. You are no thespian. You are a recognizer. You become a lover's silk hat, then topple over into THE PURE COMEDY of an infallible ray of light. That's nothing but you making an appearance. You are not a secret. You look like a metaphysician caught between a lover's dazzling white fluttering skirt and ebony waves breaking. O thoughtless thinker. You are not meaningless. As soon as one thinks one has been found out, it's THE END OF THE FIRST PART. This is not meaningless. This is not meaning. One suspects this is that thing that will never end. An icy audience in an icy cinema, just as I am about to freeze to death because of your temperature, I decide to become icy too. And I divine that when my blooming youth comes in, thawing will occur for the first time and will circulate like blood among the secluded rocks. At this moment an iridescent fern,

ように通過する。頭上の星が舌端に鏤められる時である。時間がいかにして真珠であるのか？ すべての商人すらそれを知覚するだろう。 快感が宇宙に遍在するだろう。 快感のために絶叫する枝垂柳よ、ぼくは快感のために汝をここに記入する。 太陽氏よ、君は空想ではない。 意味ではない。無意味ではない。 鳥ではない。 人ではない。 ぼくが記述のために疲れてまどろむ時驚くべきほど近くの水平線を宝船が通過する。 ぼくは眠りに落ちた島のロビンソンであるのだろうか？ ぼくはコダックのように、暗黒の鉱石となってあらゆる影像を夢みるのであろうか？ 突然に冒険の衝動が訪れたのはこのような不可浸透のメカニスムのなかであった。 人智の結晶である夢それは名のみが夢である夢。 月光のような円柱に支えられた精神界の王よ、常に名だけが似る。 太陽氏よ君の理性は海賊襲来的である。 眩惑する五色の日光の下で機械的な宝船はたちまちに包囲された。 五色の眼をした海賊女王はエレクトロンを常食として時代錯誤的な無数の劫奪品に陶酔する。 劫掠に満ちた常春の海洋、それは君の純粋理性の領域である。 物語精神の微分子王子が極光を放射しながら馴鹿を駆って自由に交通する隔世的現在に春の海辺に出て靄の城を築いた時縦横無盡に薔薇が疾駆した。 ぼくはたちまち過去を喪失して大理石面の夢のなかに美しい衣服を

which is a golden angel, passes like an airplane through an icy door for the first time. It's the hour when stars overhead become inlaid on the tip of a tongue. How can time be a pearl? Even every shopkeeper will perceive it. Delight will be ubiquitous in the universe. O weeping willow that shouts out for delight, I write thee down here for delight. O Mr. Sun, you are not a fantasy. Not meaning. Not meaninglessness. Not bird. Not human. When I get tired from writing and nod off, a treasure ship passes by on the horizon, which is surprisingly close. Am I a Robinson who has fallen asleep on the island? Do I, like a Kodak camera, become the dark ore and dream up every shadowy image? Suddenly the impulse for adventure arrived within that inviolable psychological mechanism. The dream, a crystallization of human knowledge, is only a dream in name. O king of that mental universe supported by shafts of moonlight, a name only ever resembles. Mr. Sun, your intellect is that of a highjacking pirate. In a dazzling five-color sunbeam, a wind-up treasure ship quickly gets enclosed. A pirate queen with five-colored eyes living on electrons and getting drunk on myriad outdated spoils. The sea of everlasting spring, filled with booty, that's the realm of your pure intellect. When a castle of mist was built on the shore of spring in the cross-generational present by a molecular prince of the soul of a story—driving a reindeer and freely traveling back and forth while radiating an aurora—a rose was freely running

拾う。 白い馬が無関係に走る。 屡々ぼくの指と太陽氏よ君の指との間を走るのは楽しい。 雨が君のなかにある時、雪がぼくのなかにある。 未解決の大理石の急湍のなかに白い夢が浮かぶ。 太陽氏は夢を結ぶ。 純白の瓶のなかに夢を結ぶ。 純白の秘密は永遠に純白に包まれて純白の夢を結ぶ。太陽氏よ、君の軽羅のような贈物は超経験の隕石である。 それはぼくの純白の胸を叩く。 霰の碑銘は純白の中心を遊泳し、金羊毛の海賊が眠っている。 見給え、太陽氏よ、君の永眠の上に純白の鶴が舞う。 君の永眠の帯青色の部分に愛藏された鯉の謔語が球形の虚偽を告白する。 ぼくは何も知らないものではないのだ。 たとえば君の出入する扉口。 君のネオンの寝台は無限の眼で装飾されている。 無限の時間の遭遇の眺望、眼ざめた金剛石の潜水夫‥

(未完)

about. I soon forget the past and pick up some beautiful clothes from inside a marble-surfaced dream. An unrelated white horse runs by. Fun is often running between your fingers and mine, Mr. Sun. When it's raining inside you, it's snowing inside me. A white dream floats in a torrent of insoluble marble. Mr. Sun gets tied up with a dream. Gets tied up with a dream in a snow-white bottle. A snow-white secret is then wrapped up in snow-white forever and gets tied up with a snow-white dream. Mr. Sun, your gossamer present is like a super-empirical meteorite. And it beats up my snow-white chest. A hail-written inscription floats at the center of snow-white, and the pirate with the Golden Fleece sleeps. Look, Mr. Sun, how snow-white cranes are dancing above your eternal rest. A carp's verbal baiting, cherished in the blue band of your eternal rest, confesses to global deception. It doesn't mean I don't know anything. For example, the door by which you come in and go out. Your neon bed is decorated with infinite eyes. The prospect of a chance meeting in infinite time, a now wide-awake diver of diamonds . . .

(unfinished)

Seven Poems

七つの詩

サルバドール　ダリ

　ながい縞の叫びが
　生ぶ毛のある小石たちの眼をさます
　虚空のあばたは
　制服の蝶のように
　月のような女の顔
　頭のない顔に
　今宵かなしくもとまった
　不眠のベンチの
　時計たちは
　湖水からあがった両棲類であった
　地球儀はいま
　烈しいノスタルジーに罹り
　空間は怖ろしい欲望に満ち
　三角定規のように固く顫動する
　歴史的な夕焼けのなかに
　人間は抱き合う
　飢えた臆病な小雀の群れは
　怖ろしい二十世紀物體の
　大スペクタクルのあいだに舞い降りる
　それは宇宙の容器であり内容である

Salvador Dalí

The howl of a long band
wakes the downy pebbles
A pockmarked abyss
is a woman's moony face
sadly perched tonight
like a uniformed butterfly
on a headless face
Clocks
on sleepless benches
were amphibians out of lake water
Now the globe
suffers from severe nostalgia
and space, filled with a frightening desire,
quivers rigidly like a triangle
In the glow of the historic sunset
humans hold onto one another
Flocks of timid famished sparrows
fly down amid the grand spectacle
of terrifying twentieth-century objects
It is the container and contents of the universe

純粋な幼児たちの
驚嘆のコンプレックス
巨大なチャック鞄グランドピアノは
大口をあいた假面である
Dali　という字に沿って
蝕まれた不思議な海岸がよこたわる
ダリ　それはぞっとさせる波音である

The fascinating complexes

of pure infants

The gigantic zipper-bag grand piano

is a mask with a wide-open mouth

Alongside the letters *D a l í*

lies a mysterious eroded shoreline

Dalí   the eerie sound of the waves

マックス　エルンスト

夜の旅行者は
不可解な夜の手錠を
肉片のように
食い散らす

声のない夜半に
ゴビ砂漠気附で届く
擬態の手紙がある

言葉の鑵詰を
飢えた永遠の鳥たちは
肉片と間違えるのだ

一夜
人間の贈り物は
花のように燃えていた

Max Ernst

Night tourists
gobble up
night's cryptic handcuffs
as if they were bits of T-bone

At voiceless midnight
mimed letters arrive
C/O THE GOBI DESERT

Famished immortal birds
mistake a tin can of words
for a tiny morsel of meat

One night
a human gift
was flaming like a flower

ルネ　マグリット

解放された影絵
絶えず水のように流れる
走馬燈のようにいそいで
山と山のあいだを流れる
北極の孤独は
人間の影絵たちで賑わう
絶えず発信するＡＢＣ

ぼろぼろに裂けた岸辺で
一個のシルクハットが燃える
鏡のいたずらのように
人間の木魂のように
無限にシルクハットを焼く
そして炎たちは
ＡＢＣのように受信された

美しい月蝕の夜に
影絵たちは微笑した

René Magritte

Liberated silhouettes
flow continuously like water
flow between mountains
rushing like a kaleidoscope
The loneliness of the North Pole
bustles with human silhouettes
Endlessly transmitted A B C

On the tattered shore
a single top hat burns
like a mirror trick
like a human echoing
infinitely burns a top hat
And the flames
were received as A B C

On the night of a beautiful lunar eclipse
the silhouettes smiled

ホアン　ミロ

風の舌
いつも晴れているコバルトの空が
嚙みついた
あなたの絵
太古のポスターのなかで
言葉たちが小石のようにまどろむ

羽毛のギャロップ
荒繩と猛獸たちの会話を
誘拐する
天国と地獄の結婚を
あなたは瞬ばたくほくろのなかにえがく
鏡のなかのリボンを結ぶよりも
速かに

子供たちの廣場
転がる球に紛れて飛ぶ
一つの透明な球
それをミロと呼ぶ

Joan Miró

The tongue of the wind
The always clear cobalt-blue sky
nibbled away at
your painting
In a stone age poster
words doze like pebbles

A gallop of feathers
abducts
the discourse between coarse ropes and cutthroat animals
You paint inside a blinking mole
the marriage of heaven and hell
quicker than
tying a ribbon in a mirror

A seesaw playground
From a mass of rolling balls
one seen-through ball flies off
I call it Miró

パブロ　ピカソ

飛ぶ鳥たちの
悲しげな眼も
歌のように
ひとびとの血液のなかに釘づけになる
水のなかの瞳や唇は
土のなかの耳や額に呼びかける
風のなかの愛は
やさしい声をあげて
花瓣の窓を開ける
白い椅子は黒い脚を曲げて
刀のように
乳房を刺す

月の出に
女は素肌に眼を落す
血ぬられた地図は
青く拡ろがり
水鳥の翅は
海をかくす
乳の色はかすかに
血の色をかくす

Pablo Picasso

The sorrowful eyes
of soaring birds
get hammered into our blood
like songs
The pupils and lips in water speak
to ears and foreheads in earth
Love in the air
raises a tender voice
and opens wide the petals' window
A white chair bends its black legs
and sword-like
impales the woman's chest

At moonrise
the woman drops her eyes to her bare skin
A map smeared with blood
spreads its blue
and the wings of waterbirds
conceal the ocean
The color of milk partly obscures
the color of blood

マン　レイ

解剖された月
光りの歯たちが
光りの肋骨たちに出会う

肉體に影の恋人たちが住む
ささやきが大きな眼のなかの
無限の階段で聴こえる
美しい言葉が
水晶の大きな眼のなかで
光りの鳥たちに変形する
美しい光のみの豹が逆立ちする
あらゆる星たちが衣服に棲まる

光りの裸體
彫像にほのぼのと
血液がはしるだろう

Man Ray

A dissected moon
The white teeth of light
meet the light's ribs

Shadow-lovers live inside the body
Listen to whispers
on an infinite staircase inside an enormous eye
Lovely words
transform into birds of light
inside gigantic crystal oculi
Panthers all out of lovely light are standing on their hands
All the stars reside inside outfits

Light's naked body
Warm blood could run
faintly through a statue

イヴ　タンギー

重量のないピストルか
あなたの手は

けむりの尻尾は
盡きない会話のように
開花と死の危険を犯す
砂漠のあたま
空白は櫛目ただしく這う
晴雨計はまばたきもなく
夢を追った
放たれた小豚は
薔薇の耳をかしげながら
星のように消えた

あらゆる人たちは
あらゆる人たちを待つ
未知の
けれども見覚えのある
無窮の將棋盤の上で

Yves Tanguy

Is it a weightless pistol
your hand

A tail of smoke
like an endless conversation
risks blooming and death
The head of a desert
Blanks follow the parallel lines made by a comb
A barometer pursued its dream
without even blinking
The just-released piglet
pricked up its pink rose-petal ears
and disappeared like a shooting star

Everyone
waits for everyone else
on an unknown
and yet familiar
never-ending chessboard.

花籠に充満せる人間の死

　人間がいるために花籠が曲がる。　揺れる。　破裂する。その日光を浴びて透明なパイプを握って煙を吹く。　私の指の水平線に美神が臍を出して泳ぐ。　おお否認された白梅のほうを向けよ人間の鮮明な心臓の見える人間の青い縞を見たまえ。　人間の厳かな縞の腕をナイアガラ瀑布まで延ばせ。　その上の遥かな天で無類の鯛を釣れ!　落下する瀑布に飾られた美しい虚空の花籠、それよりも美しい花籠。　いますこし頸を曲げる、いますこし眼をあげる、見よ美しい花籠はぼくの乗った花籠である。

　いま美人を切ったところである。　ほとばしる月光のような血を見よ。　彼女の喉の機械を見よ。　さて私は眠る。突貫する白鳥と、ひとつの顔を無数の星のように振る馬はこれは何か? これは美人の眼鏡であるか。

The Flower Basket Filled with Human Death

Because there are humans, the flower basket is bent. It rocks back and forth. It bursts open. Now, I'm bathing in its sunlight and holding a see-through pipe and blowing smoke. The Goddess of Beauty swims toward the horizon of my fingers, her navel exposed. O turn to the plum tree whose white blossoms have now been relinquished, look up at the human blue streaks that reach out to where a vivid human heart can be seen. Stretch out a solemn striated human arm toward Niagara Falls. In the far-off sky above, fish for an incomparable sea bream! There is the flower basket of the beautiful void decorating the cascading waterfall, and an even lovelier flower basket. Now tilt your head back a bit, now raise your eyes a little and look: that lovely flower basket is the one I'm riding in.

I have just cut off a beautiful woman. See blood like a flood of moonlight. See the machinery of her throat. Now I will sleep. What's this, a swan charging in and a horse shaking its face as if there were countless stars? Are these the woman's glasses?

これが無病な人間の凱旋門であるなら、その股のモン・ブランを風車のように突風に当てよ。突風の鮮明な顔に美粧を施して見よ。

　山査子のほかにはどんな本體も考えられないのか。　ヒトデはひとりの汝を照らし四人の汝を照らすとき、乾物屋は一層妖艶な大使を照らす。　大使の円運動はオレンジ色である。大使を慰めたのちに私は黄金の麦酒を飲む。　それから空中に浮かぶ禁断の金魚を射落す。　それから馬のように夏々と駆けてゆく。　が待て、ひとりの詩神は冷たくなっている。

　深海の突進する機関車を着て、廊下で濃藍色のヴィーナスを転ろがす。　ダビデのような比目魚の横顔は直接背後の珊瑚色の象を知らない。　この鬚に満ちた男は人間に復れと命じている。　潜望鏡にうつった紅梅を熟視せよ。ダビデよ。無数に波頭が死ぬ。

　純粋な男がなんとなく左手を右手に合わせている。　これは純粋な行為であった。　それから特に清浄な太陽に宝石を飾るために空中に浮かんでいた。　人間に復った人間が真実の紫陽花色をした現実を嚙った瞬間は名誉ある鰐の全世界であった。　これは衰弱の萬歳である。　石礆で洗滌した鮮やかな鰐の眼よ。　改めて花籠の純粋な自然を見よ。　棕梠の葉

If this is the triumphal arch of a disease-free human, let a blast of wind blow against this mons's Mont Blanc, as if it were a windmill. Try to beautify the vivid face of a gust of wind.

Can you think of no other trunk but that of a hawthorn? While a starfish lights up "thee" and four other "thee"s, a dried-fish monger lights up a captivating ambassador even more. The ambassador's circular motion is the color of an orange. After consoling him, I drink a golden pale ale. And then shoot down a taboo goldfish floating in the air. And then gallop clip-clop like a horse. But wait, one of the Muses has grown cold.

In the deep sea, wearing a speedy locomotive, I roll a blue-dyed Venus in a hallway. The olive flounder's David-like profile is unaware of the coral-pink elephant standing behind it. This unshaved man demands, Go back to being a human being. Look hard through the periscope at the red plum blossoms. O David. The countless cresting waves die down.

A pure man puts the palm of his left hand against that of his right hand for no apparent reason. This was a pure gesture. That then soared through the air to adorn the immaculate sun with precious stones. When the human who had returned to being human took a bite out of a true hydrangea-colored reality, that moment was the whole world for an upstanding crocodile. This is a hooray for weakness. O bright crocodile eyes washed out with soap. Look again at pure nature in the flower basket. O

にダイヤモンドを鏤ばめる独特の潜水夫よ。 汝の摩天楼の胴よ。 私を抱け！ 純粋な脳髄よ。 鰐を通せ！ 征服された菫は巡洋艦のごとく大洋に横たわる。 同じように征服された雁を見よ。 その紫の神が墜落する。 その嫋やかな神が七絃琴に衝突したとき、獅子の口蓋の肉片のように消失してしまった。 このオペラを見よ。 そこに歓喜する美神を見よ。 星の魅惑に打ちわななく平原、そこに木炭が似合うのは鯉の霊感であった。 最愛のスペクトラムよ。 叢生の萩のしたの無限の銅鉱に独特な容貌をあたえよ。 すべての愛は汝を通って光る。すべての死もまた汝を通って光る。 雷鳴のなかにいる一人の娘よ。 小麦畑の葉末に華やかな突然の神々を信ぜよ。

unique diver who inlays diamonds in palm leaves. O thy highrise torso. Embrace me! O pure brain. Make way for the crocodile! A conquered violet lies on the ocean's surface like a cruiser. Take a gander at a similarly overcome wild goose. That purple god fell. When that graceful god collided with a seven-string zither, it vanished like a scrap of tenderloin off a lion's palate. Look at this opera. Look over there at the delighted Goddess of Beauty. That disquieted plain, captivated by the stars, was what gave the koi the bright idea that lignite would make quite a nice match. O dearest spectrum! Give singular features to that infinite vein of copper ore under a growth of bush clover. All love passes by thee and glistens. All dying passes through thee and also glistens. O one girl inside a thunderclap. Trust in the sudden flamboyant gods at the tiptop of a wheat field's leaves.

amphibia

種子の魔術のための幼年

ひとつの爆発をゆめみるために幼年のひたいに崇高な薔薇いろの果実をえがく

パイプの突起で急に寂しがる影をもたぬ雀を注意ぶかく見まもる

井戸のような瞳孔の頭の幼い葡萄樹はついに悦ぶ

金魚は死を拒絶した

雨のふる太陽

かれの頸環の晴天

amphibia

childhood as the magic seed's offspring

depicting a sublime rose-colored fruit on the forehead of
childhood in order to imagine an implosion

carefully tending to a shadowless sparrow that's suddenly
lonely on the swollen bowl of a pipe

the infantile grapevine with inkwell pupils is finally
delighted

the golden-hamlet-fish refused to say yes to dying

the sun's rainfall is falling on

his convertible-collar's clear weather

ポール　エリュアールに

à Paul Eluard

1

天使よ、この海岸では透明な悪魔が薔薇を抱いている。薔薇
の頭髪の薔薇色は悪魔の奇蹟。珊瑚のダイナモに倚りかかり
おまえの立っているのは砂浜である。神が貝殻に隠れたまう
とき破風に悪魔の薔薇色の影がある。それは正午である。

2

やさしい鳥が窓に衝突する。それは愛人の窓である。暗黒の
真珠貝は法典である。墜落した小鳥は愛人の手に還る。蝸牛
を忘れた処女は完全な太陽を残して死ぬ。舞踏靴は星のよう
にめぐる。

To Paul Éluard

à Paul Éluard

1

Angel, on this shore a transparent devil embraces a rose. The rose color of the rose's hair is the devil's miracle. You stand idly by, leaning against a coral generator on a sandy beach. When a god is hiding in a seashell, the devil's rosy shadow is lying on a gable. It is high noon.

2

A gentle birdie collides with a window. This is a lover's window. Inside a dark pearl oyster shell, one finds a body of laws. The downfallen birdie returns to the lover's hands. A maid who has mislaid a snail dies, leaving behind an impeccable sun. Dancing shoes circle like stars.

MIROIR DE MIROIR　鏡の鏡

　櫻の灰の姿見には櫻の足跡がある。　昔、小石の耳をもった小鳥が林の姿見に墜落、永遠の未来の孤独のみみずくよ、汝の裸體は黄金の硝子かと見まごう、大火災ベルリンに起る、みみずくよ聞きたまえ。　ぼくの同情はすべて詩であった。　みみずくの児童らよ、九人目の童女の眉の上にあって最も光る電燈は何なのかね？　この小石等の笑うのを聞きたまえ。明日の冬に無数の愛の雪が降るのが見えるかね？　小麦の幻想は年々変化して美少女の扮装のように年々麗わしくなる。　金魚を嗅ぐ機械によって心臓のように精巧な水路のなかに雪が降っていることを知った。　小麦の乾く鏡のなかに鯨の骨骼が朝の太陽のように動く。　美少女の磁石のごとく動く。　小麦は動揺する。　小麦の石の乳房は鯖の女優の鏡である。そこに波を描いていった豊艶な雀はぼくの掌に眠っていた。　ぼくの指から飛びたつもっとも美しい紫の小鳥は巣に帰る。　綻び

MIROIR DE MIROIR: MIRRORED MIRROR

The footprints of the cherry tree appear in the full-length mirror of the cherry tree's ashes.   Long ago, a little birdie with pebble ears fell through the mirror of the forest, O solitary owl of the endless future, thy naked body could be mistaken for golden glass, listen owl, A CONFLAGRATION IS OCCURRING IN BERLIN.   My compassion was all in verse.   O kiddos of the owl, what is that light bulb shining most brightly above the ninth girl's eyebrows? Listen to that gravel laugh.   Can you see the snow of countless loves falling in the winter of tomorrow?   The illusion of a wheat field changes with each passing year, becoming, like the costumes of a beautiful girl, more and more lovely.   Through a device that can detect the scent of a goldfish, I came to know it was snowing in a waterway as convoluted as the heart.   In the mirror where the wheat field is drying, the skeleton of a whale rises like the morning sun.   Moves like the magnet of a beautiful belle.   The wheat is stirring.   The wheat's stone breasts act as a mirror of the mackerel actress.   The voluptuous sparrow that drew the waves there, then left, was sleeping in my hand.   The loveliest little lavender birdie set off from my fingers and flew back to its nest. The fish mending the ripped coast with gold thread are drinking

た岸に金糸の縫いをする魚たちは雲間の温湯を飲む。 ゼロの孔雀は黄色の鏡から水を吸い、百萬長者の瀑布は木兎の頭の白い帆船を包むだろう。 それは無限の時間の無限に白色のペリカンの再生、ふしぎに乳房、これは銅と木兎を育てた大森林の乳である。 黒雲の乳星の乳、

　ぼくの七つの鏡を産んだ鳩の婦人は午前のぼくの乳を吸う。ぼくの鏡の牧草はいまは鳩の胸よりも高く成長して蝶々の脳髄をいただく、その両足のあいだの闇の鳩たちの心臓は交互的である。接吻の花が梅の花の上にひらく。鳩の婦人の裸體の時刻、氷山が語る時刻、ひとでが笑う時刻である。四面岩壁にかこまれた青い鰈の美しい音声を聴きたまえ、ぼくの瞳のなかの木兎の児童らよ。汝らの皮膚の暦の装飾よ。天の愛情は沼の底のシャンデリヤと鯉の可愛い手袋にそそぐ。黄金の宝の黄金は汝の頬のなかの絵一個の天體一個の符号白熊OUI

　湖の上の七つの完全な自然よ波紋の肋骨の動物に跨った無限の太陽の艶麗な胸は彼らの習慣のとおりに花を挿している。雲に包まれた雷鳴の秘密の心臓の美神はさぼてんの花に姻戚関係。ぼくの組んだ手の川の波、ぼくの牝鶏の声が一、

from the warm springs in the space between clouds. Zero's peacock will sip water from a yellow mirror, and the millionaire's waterfall will shroud the white canvas sail on the owl's head. It's the rebirth of white pelicans in the timelessness of infinite time and, oddly, breasts: the milk of the enormous forest that wet-nursed copper and owls. Black cloud milk, star milk,

In the morning, I breastfeed the lady-doves who gave birth to my seven mirrors. The meadow grasses in my mirror are now higher than the doves' breasts and are given butterfly brains; between their legs, the doves of darkness exchange hearts. The flower's kiss blooms on a plum blossom. It's time for the lady-doves' naked bodies, the time for icebergs to talk, the time for starfish to laugh. O children of the owl in my pupils, listen to the beautiful voice of the blue flounder surrounded on four sides by stone parapets. O the ornaments on the calendar of thy skin. Heavenly love pours into the chandelier at the bottom of the marsh and into the koi's adorable gloves. The gold of gold treasure is a painting on thy cheek, one celestial body, one sign, an icy polar bear's OUI.

O seven perfect natures on the lake straddling animals with rippling ribs, infinite suns wearing flowers on their ravishing chests, each according to its custom. The Goddess of Beauty of the cloud-wrapped secret heart of thunder is related by marriage to the cactus flower. The waves of the river in my cupped hands,

紅玉であり、二、大理石である膝、窓から見える湖水の上の船の花、自然石である少年が地下水のような雲のしたの波のしたの鯉の幼児に叩頭する。ぼくは急行列車のなかで宝石の野原である。これは菜の花の空中。祭礼の雲の菓子らよ、天降りせよ、微風の頬に吊りさがったボンボンボン‥‥‥両頬の円形の湖水の上の鳥の彫像は永遠である。陸上の水にうつった天の湖水の船、そのある化粧室の薔薇に扮したぼくは無限に背の高い水夫である。紫陽花の記念像を白い急の波が打壊わす最新の愛情。雪の夢の文明が彼の妖精の指輪に出現する天使の卵形の寝室は水平線に青く繁っている。妖精よ汝の妖精を愛せよ。

my hen's voice is (1) a ruby; (2) marble knees, a flower boat on the lake seen from a window, a natural-stone boy kowtows to a newborn koi beneath the waves, beneath some underwatery clouds. Inside the express train, I'm a field of gemstones. This air of yellow rapeseed blossoms. O festival cloud candies, descend from on high, bonbons hanging *boom-boom-boom* from the cheeks of the breezes . . . the sculpted figure of a bird on the cheeks' circular lakes is everlasting. I am an infinitely tall sailor disguised as the rose inside the powder room of a ship on heavenly lake water mirrored on the surface of an inland lake. The white rapids demolish the memorial hydrangea statue, the latest lovefest. The angel's ovoid bedroom, where a civilization dreamt by the snow is now appearing on his fairy ring, flourishes and turns green on the horizon. O fairy love thy fairy.

岩石は笑った

狂った世紀の墓標のための
鉄の帽子湧きでたためしのない噴水塔は
蝶の幽霊揚げられたためしのない幕を
狂った歌を叫びながら追ってゆく
壊われた夕闇みの貝殻のなかの
若い女たちの頰のえくぼを踏みにじった人間たちは
彼らの自由永遠に濡れない海綿停まった振子正四面體
　　の心臓をもつ
裂けた眞夜中に裂けた犠牲たちに
人間の脳は沸きたつ花瓶となる
猿たち共同墓地
乾いたパン屑不完全な家具貝殻のカフェは沸きたつ
星は太陽と交接する紫色の精液それは広漠たる明星網
　　膜の公園
闇の爆音のなかにひとつの偉大な夕顔がひらく奇妙な髭
　　男が笑う

The Rock Cracked Up

As a headstone for a mad century,
a cast iron hat. A tower fountain that never flowed
is the ghost of a butterfly tracing a stage curtain that has
    never been raised
while shouting an insane song.
Humans who trampled on the dimples
of young women in the shell of a broken dusk have their
    freedom,
never-wetted sea sponges, stopped metronomes, and
    tetrahedral hearts.
At torn-apart midnight for the shredded victims
the human braincase becomes a boiling vase.
Monkeys, graveyards.
Stale breadcrumbs, imperfect furniture, seashell cafés are
    boiling with excitement.
A star's lavender gametes mate with the sun, it's the huge
    morning star, a public park of the retina.
As the darkness explodes one magnificent moonflower
    opens, a strange bearded man bursts out laughing.

夢の室内に星の破片と卓子の破片とで

巨大な女は巨大な匙で組みたてる地球美しい花飾り

時の不可分の瞬間に

蹄の音がするてのひらの電波落葉の手袋手袋の優しい風

蹄は日光の石を粉砕して

埃のなかに無数の不眠の鳥たちを追放する

記憶はけむりの猫を生み

それは突然な無関心な男ひとりの男の指輪一挺の水晶
　　拳銃は

両国橋の下とぼくの寝床白い布の下とに

ひとつの運命を狙う

扉から投げられる広告紙朝の波紋から

断髪の女は白象と一緒に

ぼくの歯ブラシの上に落ちる

悲しげな朝の

長い旅行古代からの旅行の不調和な影像たち石鹸無効
　　切符首府の夜景

美釘の抜けた美通り魔の解剖図

In the room of a dream made of bits of stars and splinters of
   tables
a gigantic woman constructs an earth with an extra-large
   ladle, a beautiful floral ornament.
In an indivisible moment of time
the sound of hooves is heard in the palms' radio waves, the
   gloves of fallen leaves, a gentle breeze of gloves.
The hooves pulverize the sunlit stones
and chase countless insomniac birds into the dust.
Recollection gives rise to a smoke cat.
Suddenly it's an indifferent man, one man's ring, one crystal
   handgun
beneath Ryogoku Bridge and under my bed's snow-white
   cover
taking aim at one fate.
From the morning ripples of leaflets thrown from a door
a bob-haired woman with a white elephant
topples over onto my toothbrush.
A sad morning's
long trip. The discordant shadows of a journey that leads
   back to ancient times, soap bar, ticket stubs, the night
   view of the capital.
The lovely killer's anatomy chart where the lovely nails have
   all been pulled out.

それは風の小便にほかならない

ゴム輪が鳥たちの衣服になれば

闇のなかの鳥たちはぼくの睫毛となる

微かな不思議な條件が宇宙の決意から

理髪師の小器用な小指の上に輝いている

指のピラミッドの上の春の太陽

誰も想像しえないで

夢の特急列車はえにしだの上を走る

誰も探りえないで

牝牛は足跡にひとつひとつの眞珠を残す

法衣はいま激烈な小便で酩酊している

雨白い雨は百合の花莖を膨らませ

姙娠した聖母は排気鐘のなかで他愛なく眠る

長い夢の鳥の尾は明滅する

すべての朝は星の呼鈴を押す

すべての朝は自分で自分を洗う

すべての顔すべての空に自由の水が流れる

雨たちの指が二十日鼠の指に似るとき

ぼくはぼくのシャツの星のボタンを掛ける

ぼくはぼくの耳が偉大な想像の瀧の薔薇を聴くために

千年一度の形體であるとき

河のように流れる

It's nothing but pissing in the wind.

If an elastic band becomes the larks' glad rags

larks in the dark become my eyelashes.

The universe causes a subtle mysterious proviso

to glitter on the pinkie finger of the skilled barber.

The spring sun on the finger-raised pyramid.

Unable to dream someone up

the dream's limited express runs on common broom.

Unable to seek someone out

a moo-cow drips out pearls one by one in its footprints.

Now the priest's robe gets intensely pissed on piss.

Rain-white rain swells the stem of a lily

and a pregnant Madonna sleeps well in a bell jar.

The fantail of a bird flickers in a long dream.

Each morning depresses a star's doorbell.

Each morning washes itself off by itself.

From every face, from every sky, the waters of freedom flow.

When the rain's fingers look like the mitts of mice

I button up the stars of my shirt.

So that my ears will hear the rose of a grand imaginary
     waterfall

when it takes a form that occurs once in a thousand years,

I go with the flow like a river.

大象徴の前にタブーの大旅行鞄の前に
疲れて投げだした巨大な足の溜息巨大な自由の通風筒
　が数える
秒音音楽的な秒音
さて眞夜中の諢語太陽のスカートは永遠に凋まない

In front of a supersized symbol, in front of a taboo
　　supersized suitcase,
the sigh of enormous legs wearily stretching out, free
　　gigantic ventilating shafts counting
the sound of seconds, the musical sound of seconds.
Now for a midnight wisecrack, the sun's skirt is never going
　　to [a] shrink.

Fairy's Distance

妖精の距離

蝸牛の劇場

白と黒の窓がひらく
蝸牛の眼は見た
あるときはうつくしい目だけを
あるときは青いリボンだけを
あるときはシガレットの灰だけを
そして彼は恋をした

ひっそりしたトリトンの噴水!

夜半　だしぬけに大きな掌が翻った
トランプのように華やかに
太陽が彼の純粋な眼を盗んだ
いろはにほへと
彼は卵形に捩れている

The Snail's Theatrical Stage

A black and white window opens
The snail's eyes saw
Once, nothing but beautiful eyes
Once, nothing but a blue ribbon
Once, nothing but a cigarette's ash
Then he fell in love

Triton's quieted fountain!

Midnight   suddenly a large palm turned up
with the flourish of a trump card
The sun swiped his innocent eyes
ABRACADABRA
He's been twisted into an egg-shape

レダ

　突風は貝殻をコップのように空虚にする

　燈火は消された!

　月の下には禁獵区が白い扇のように横たわっている

　彼女の留針は休息している

　ひとりあるきは薔薇の匂いがする

　レダは吊下っている!

Leda

A gust of wind turns the shell into an empty glass

The light's been blown out!

Under the moon the no-hunting zone lies like a white fan

L's straight pin is taking a rest

Walking alone has the redolence of roses

Leda is left hanging!

魚の慾望

純潔な装飾
無数の逆さ蠟燭たちの疼痛
透明な樹々の枝と花
無限大の鏡の轟きと
家々の窓々の痙攣

私の全身
一日一日輝きをましてゆく水の化石の中に
私の慾望はなおも泳ぐ
青空と呼ぶ巨大な釣燭台の落し子である私
たれも私を恋のスフィンクスと呼ばない

私の夢は碧玉の寓話のなかで
一層青く燦めいた

The Fish's Desire

Chastity ornaments
The pain of countless inverted candles
The boughs and blooms of see-through trees
The rumble of infinite mirrors
and the spasms of house windows

My undiminished body
In the fossilized water that brightens day by day
my desire still swims
I, bastard child of a huge chandelier called the blue sky
No one refers to me as the subtle sphinx of love

In a jasper fable my dream
glistened all the more blue

瞬間撮影

匂いは花と共に生きている
夜のミルクは仔牛の夢の
痩せた車輪をまわす
さかさの海の無邪気な鳥が
飢えながら光の泥をはこぶ
影のように
水のように
紫水晶の蝶がうずまく
恋文から今日も夜がすべり落ちる
幸福が今日も破れた鏡にまばたく

Snapshotting

Fragrant scents are alive at the side of lavish flowers

Nocturnal milk spins the skin-and-bones wheel

of a calf's dream

An innocent starving bird from an upside-down sea

carries off muddy light

Like shadows

like water

amethyst butterflies swirl

Today again night slips off a love letter

Today again gaiety winks in a shattered mirror

遮られない休息

跡絶えない翅の

幼い蛾は夜の巨大な瓶の重さに堪えている

かりそめの白い胸像は雪の記憶に凍えている

風たちは痩せた小枝にとまって貧しい光に慣れている

すべて

ことりともしない丘の上の球形の鏡

Undisturbed Bed Rest

With extended wings

an infantile moth bears the weight of night's mammoth bottle

A momentary white torso freezes in the recollection of snow

Breezes perched on thin twigs adapt to dim light

All

is a mirrored globe on a hill where you could hear a pin drop

木魂の薔薇

瓶の中のほのかな生命
私はお前を飲む

階段の上のそらいろの影
私はお前を踏む

愛の身振りが
シガレットの薔薇を燃やすとき
木魂が灰の中から出てきた

The Echo's Rose

Delicate life at the bottom of a bottle
I drink you up

Sky-blue shadow resting on the landing
I step up and onto to you

Whenever a gesture of love
singed the cigarette's rose
an echo of O arose from the ash

反 応

夜は

風の鏡で怖ろしい孤独のリボンを結ぶ

夜は

平面の容器の中に

星ほどの近さで

恋ほどの狭さの夜衣を縫う

眼のようにすべては明るい

眼のようにすべては見えない

蝕んだ影の彼方に

ふしぎな昆虫の光を見出す

少女のように

白い足の反応

紅い雪の反応

Reactions

Night

in the wind's hand mirror ties a ribbon of terrifying solitude

Night

as near as the stars

in a two-dimensional container

sews a nightgown as narrow as love

Like the eye everything is glistening

Like the eye everything is invisible

Far beyond a worm-eaten shadow

the light of a mysterious insect is found

Like a slip of a girl

the white legs' reaction

the red snow's reaction

睡 魔

ランプの中の噴水、噴水の中の仔牛、仔牛の中の蠟燭、蠟
　燭の中の噴水、噴水の中のランプ

私は寝床の中で奇妙な昆虫の軌跡を追っていた
そして瞼の近くで深い記憶の淵に落ちこんだ
忘れ難い顔のような
眞珠母の地獄の中へ
私は手をかざしさえすればいい
小鳥は歌い出しさえすればいい
地下には澄んだ水が流れている

卵形の車輪は
遠い森の紫の小筐に眠っていた
夢は小石の中に隠れた

Drowsiness

Fountain in a lamp, calf in a fountain, candle in a calf,
    fountain in a candle, lamp in a fountain

In bed I was following the trajectory of an odd insect
and near my eyelid fell into the deep abyss of memory
Like an unforgettable face
in some hell's mother-of-pearl shell
I only have to hold up my hand
A little birdie only has to begin singing
Clear water runs in the underground spring

An oval wheel
was asleep in a small lavender basket in a far-off forest
A dream stowed away in a pebble

影の通路

夜よ
お前の肩甲骨の中の鳩が
三色菫の夢を見るとき
何をお前は見たか?
影に打ち抜かれた壁が
ランプの唇の夢を見たとき
何をお前は見たか?

小さな食卓の
盲いた瓶たちは海鳴りがする
影は朱に染まって倒れている
そして夜の心臓のように透きとおっている
そして卵のように飢えている

The Shadow's Passage

O night
when the pigeon in your scapula
dreamed of pansies
what did you see?
When the wall bitten into by a shadow
had a dream about the lamp's lips
what did you see?

On a small dining table
blind bottles roar like the sea
A dyed-red shade has fallen down
Now seen through like the heart of night
Now greedy like an egg

妖精の距離

うつくしい歯は樹がくれに歌った
形のいい耳は雲間にあった
玉虫色の爪は水にまじった
脱ぎすてた小石
すべてが足跡のように
そよ風さえ
傾いた椅子の中に失われた
麦畑の中の扉の発狂
空気のラビリンス
そこには一枚のカードもない
そこには一つのコップもない
慾望の楽器のように
ひとすじの奇妙な線で貫かれていた
それは辛うじて小鳥の表情に似ていた
それは死の浮標のように
春の風に棲まるだろう
それは辛うじて小鳥の均衡に似ていた

Fairy's Distance

Hiding inside trees beautiful eyeteeth were singing

Between clouds a shapely ear

Iridescent nails dissolved in water

Discarded pebbles

Like footprints everything

even the wind

was getting lost in a leaning chair

A crazed entrance into a wheat field

A labyrinth made of air

There's not even one playing card

There's not a single glass

Like a stringed instrument of desire

a strange line pierced it

It just barely looked like a bird's expression

Like a death buoy it will live

in the spring wind

It just barely looked like a bird's sense of balance

風の受胎

うつくしい燈のある風が
樹の葉を灼きつくす
夜の巨大な蝶番いが
お前の若さを揺るがす

雪花石膏の夜
不滅の若さが翅のように
閉じそして開く

夢がとどろき
星の均衡が小枝から失われた

The Conception of Wind

The wind with a graceful lamp
reduces the leaves of trees to ashes
Your salad days are shaken up
by the mammoth hinge of night

On an alabaster night
everlasting youth
closes and opens like wings

A dream thundered in
and twigs lost the stability of stars

夜 曲

鳥の棲むコップから
女囚は手袋を脱ぐ
月の下の浴みは彼女に喪中の均衡を与える
夜は夜の中のすべてをくっきりと照らす
噴水は絶えずうつろな寝床の皺を縫っていた
彼女は鍵穴のように痩せている
やがて彼女は骨盤の中に自由を感じた

今日とあすのあいだの白いハンカチフ

赤い唇の永遠の休暇
太陽はコップの底に沈澱している
眠れない小鳥と一緒に

Nocturne

From a glass where swallows live

a prisoner removes her gloves

A moonlight bath gives her the equipoise of one in

   mourning

Night clearly illuminates everything inside night

A fountain kept sewing the wrinkles of the empty bed

She is as slender as a keyhole

Soon, she felt freedom in her pelvic ring

Between today and tomorrow a white handkerchief

An endless holiday of red lips

The sediment of the sun is at the bottom of the glass

together with the sleepless birds

TEXTE ÉVANGÉLIQUE

　埃っぽい自転車が燦然と虚空へ落ちてゆくのを見おろしながら、豊かな葡萄の木に凭れながら、私は嘶く。オリンポスから降りてきたこの雪の積った女神を畏れる理由がない。しかしこの機械のような岩清水は何だ。　さて私の追憶に誤りがなければその鍍金の剥げた形の崩れた美神は池の金髪と青空の血液によって、今朝、薔薇色に蘇生した。　疾走する独特な白雪の罪過。五角形の彼女の正態。そこから突然鳩のような鳥が玉葱のように完全なものを銜えて飛びたった。絶えまなく揺れる葦の美神はこの虚空に向かって意外に美しい視線を放つ。唯一の空隙である廊下に、切断されて平衡をたもっている喬木の枝の鷲の義眼への通知に透明な蒸気機関と春の苗木との撚り糸が溯る既往の歓喜がある。　実在の処女は飛ぶ鳥を縮らせ、アポロンを蒸溜水のように透明にするという過失を小波が頭上を走る自働人形の決意のうちにする。　彼

TEXTE ÉVANGÉLIQUE

While leaning against grape-laden vines, staring down at a dusty bicycle falling glitteringly into the abyss, I whinny. I see no reason to fear or revere this snowy goddess who has descended from Mount Olympus. However, what is this fresh water mechanically trickling between the rocks? Now if I recollect correctly, this misshapen goddess of beauty with her peeling gilt had her rosy color restored this morning by way of the pond's fair hair and the sky's blood. The misdeed of this peculiar rushing white snow. Her inherent pentagonal shape. Just now, a dove-like bird flew off with something as perfect as an onion in its beak. The goddess of beauty of the endlessly stirring reeds casts a surprisingly lovely glance toward this emptiness. In the passageway (the only opening), in a message sent to a glass-eyed eagle, who ever maintains his balance on a branch of a tall tree, even after it's been severed, a past joy can be traced back via the twisted thread of a translucent steam engine and a spring sapling. With the resolve of an automaton with rippling wavelets gushing from the top of its head, the actual virgin clips the wings of a flying chick and commits the mistake of making Apollo as transparent as distilled water. At the midpoint of her horizon, the righteous fingers of

女の水平線の中点に怒る美神の正しい指は薔薇の襞をとっている。 そして空想としてそれを毟っている。 そして星のように限りなく涙を垂れている。 待て、イリュミネーションのように神々しいボンボンで彼女の張った胸を飾れ！ これはとまり木の上の盛装である。 霜に打たれた掌状植物の天真爛漫である。 効能ある墜落した霰の姿見である。 そのなかに影を落す秋空の若いマリヤが雲雀につまづいて倒れたのは日本晴れの海洋の椿事であった。 マリヤ、何を見ている？ 遅延した蕾には愛らしい関節が鳴っている。月夜のモーターの音である。 そこには数十の錯誤が鳴っているが、それは胡瓜の感謝の結果である。 星空のような両手を合わせて枝のあいだから噴水のほとりまで歩いてゆき、荘厳な双殻類の内部に突っ立っている美しい二人の彼女に挨拶する。 垂れさがった無数の毛髪に投錨する。 しかし紫陽花のビルディングを迂回するのに煉瓦色の薔薇を携える。音がする。 どうぞ、昨日の写真のわたくしの肩にその薔薇を載せておいて下さいな。 この気笛のような声は合唱であった。

　けさ狩人の脚のあいだに星が隠棲しはじめる。 それは確かに、船長よ、鴛鴦の頭から遁れたものであろう。 食用の暴風が危険をおかして泡の創造者に邂逅する。 空気の薔薇に

the outraged goddess of beauty grip the folds of the rose. And pluck it, as if it's a fantasy. And she's shedding tears, as countless as stars. Wait, take holy bonbons and adorn her swollen breasts, as if with a string of lights! They're all dressed up on a perch. This has the innocence of a frostbitten fig leaf. It's the full-length mirror of a highly effective fallen hailstone. As the seasonal fall sky casts a shadow over it, the young Mary stumbled over a lark and fell—it was a startling incident in the ocean on a glorious day. Mary, what are you looking at? Awaiting buds crack their lovely joints. It's the sound of a motor on a moonlit night. There, dozens of mistakes are making noise, but that's the result of the cucumbers' gratitude. Put both hands together like a starry sky, take a walk through the boughs to a place near the fountain where two beautiful women, just standing there inside a sublime bivalve shell, are waved to. Drop an anchor in their myriad leagues of hanging hair. But bring a brick-colored rose to skirt the hydrangea building. Something is heard. Please place that T-rose on my shoulder in yesterday's retro photo. This voice, whistling like a choo-choo, was in fact a chorus.

This morning, a star begins its secluded life between a hunter's legs. It seems, Captain, the one that just escaped the mind of a mandarin duck. An edible storm risks an encounter with the creator of foam. Touching an airy rose is something a woman

触れることは女の夢想もしないことである。　しかしそれは翌朝のあらゆる新聞に報道されている。　それが女の自殺であるかのように。　さて女の驚愕から無数の千鳥がそれぞれ透明な魂をもって飛び去る。　そしてふたたび集まるのは無用の鏡のなかであろう。　それは私がくわえた麦藁に咲く薔薇であろう。　それは彼女の技術だったように見える。睡魔に襲われた太陽は満開の花を採集する。　純粋な夢の武装にもう眼覚めることを忘れた蓮の花はパラソルを海に閉じて魚類に返事をする優しい癖、岩の表皮を破って青空を見おろす小指の真摯さ、茄子茄子この理知はおそろしい光景をあたえる。茄子と茄子とは午前零時の真理をさえ理解したのだ。　いま一度引金をひくことの花粉に遭遇せよ。　やがてきみの横顔に私の郵便集配人が到着するだろう。　松のグラスに椿事をそそぐ。　これは私が階段を歩く理由である。　あらゆる空瓶の底はそれぞれ相違する美しい天性を有する。蝸牛のリラに鑢をかける妙な天使を一瞬間以上証明するための望遠鏡となる（これはひとつの雰囲気である）。これは愛人のための計算である。

　木炭のなかへ消える潜水夫は疾走する花束を握っている。汝の體内に時計の血が流れている。　帆のある婦人は分秒毎に組織を変える。　堅い紺青の海面を破ってひと枝の薔薇の

wouldn't dream of. Yet the next morning, it's reported in all the papers. As if she'd committed suicide. Then, to her shock, countless plovers fly away, each with a transparent soul. Only to meet up again in a useless mirror. It must be the rose blooming on the straw I hold in my mouth. It appears that was her technique. The drowsy sun gathers flowers in full bloom. Armed with a pure dream, the lotus flower forgets about getting up, closes its parasol in the sea and gently nods to the fish, a mere habit; a sincere little pinkie breaks through the surface skin of a rock and looks down to see blue sky—an eggplant eggplant—this reasoning offers a terrifying sight. Eggplant and eggplant have even grasped the truth of midnight. Once again, a face-off with the pollen that pulls the trigger. My mailman will soon arrive at your side-view. And pour startling incidents into an evergreen glass. It's for this that I take the stairs. The bottom of each empty bottle has its own uniquely beautiful inborn character. And becomes a telescope that makes it possible to prove that a strange angel is using a file on a lilac snail for longer than one minute (it's someone's impression). It's a lover's calculation.

A deep-sea diver disappears into charcoal as he grasps at a bouquet flying past. In thy body, the blood of a clock keeps running. A lady with a canvas sail reforms her formation, minute by minute—breaking the stony surface of the deep-blue sea and

ような潜水夫を汲み取る。　その指と指とのあいだに夢を見た痕跡があるなら、婦人はもう一度鶯のように鳴く。　その無限に巧みな歌を鳴く！　そして即日潜水夫を海底に返還する。この沈着崇高な非金属は月のほかに眺めるものをもたない。甲冑のほかに着るものがない。秋の月光を遅延させるほかに婦人はなすすべを知らない。　それは雲雀の飛び立つ安全地帯か、婦人はそこに立って光る自動車の通過をいつまでも眺めつくす。　山査子が花盛りである。　それは婦人の全骨骼である。　王子の叫ぶ隣室の瀑布である。　リボンの結び目は太陽に融ける氷河の春景色である。　天に突起する紫のアヤメの白色の限界に婦人よ静かに眠れ。　そしてダイヤの光る指と海老とを区別するがよい。　この祝うべき時に足がもはや水底に届かない。　この近くに瑞徴のダリヤが咲く。　その香気とたたかってもっとも愛する香水の論理に還元する。　ずっと下の枝には婦人がもっとも愛する白い花が咲き零れているが婦人の指はもうそれには触れない。潜水夫の柔軟なステッキもそれを動かすことはできない。　すべての疑問のうちに夕暮れが訪れるのは残念である。　そして婦人の小鳥の乳房と潜水夫の星の爪で考える。　これは不幸であるのか、月夜であるのかと。　天空の生ぶ毛をもった天使は早くも死去してい

scooping up the diver, as if he were a spray of roses. If there is any trace of a dream inside those fingers then the lady sings a second time like a warbler. Singing that infinitely ingenious tune! And sends the diver scrambling back to the seabed that very same day. That cool-headed, sublime, nonmetal has nothing to look at except the moon. Nothing to wear except armor. The lady doesn't know any other way, other than delaying the fall's flood of moonlight. Is this the traffic island from which the larks fly off; she stands there endlessly staring at the glowing cars passing by. The hawthorn tree is in full bloom. That's her whole skeleton. It's the waterfall in the next room where a prince is shouting. A knot in the ribbon is a spring landscape where a glacier is melting in the sun. Sleep quietly, lady, at the white edge of the purple iris jutting up toward heaven. And distinguish a finger with a spar-kling diamond on it from a shrimp. In this moment, which should be celebrated, the feet no longer touch the bottom of the water. Auspicious dahlias bloom nearby. Resisting their perfume, and reducing them to the logic of a favorite fragrance. Far below the high branches, the white flowers she loves best are blossoming everywhere but her fingers can no longer reach them. The diver's flexible cane can't move them either. It's a pity that an evening comes into every question. Thinking about the woman's little birdie breasts and the diver's starry fingernails. Whether this is a misfortune or an evening of moonlight. The angel with heavenly

る。　ただ列んだ棒杭に凭れたサボテンの洗濯に一身を捧げる処女がその眼に虹のような受胎告知を受ける。　彼女も人並みにいれずみをした花をもっている。　彼女の見える梢の花への使節は独り言で有名である。　彼女の最新風俗は毟った櫻の花瓣と毟った膝とを混同して満月の引金をひくことである。　それで達しえた天国の一部分は彼女が発見しえなかった雲雀の卵が置かれてある椅子それは赤色電燈を浴びて微風にそよいでいるにすぎないのだが、彼女を待ちあぐむ素質のある彼女の全世界。　金色の空鑵に秘めていた彼女の日の出である。　また石鹸が一時のヴィーナスであるときその特有の眼と耳とがそれぞれ悲哀の調子を帯びているのを雛の嘴でつつきながら北風に刺繍する。　彼女は名勝地の波を賞める。　彼女は松の毬果の製造者である。　彼女はまっすぐに舞い降りてひとりの美女の側で難なく捕えられる。　千萬の新事実は白砂の魅力のなかに被除数のように晴れ着を着て坐っている。　それは彼女に柔順な鶴の群棲にほかならない。　それは黒玉の難破である。　彼女はいかに巧みに鳥を捉えることができるか。　いかに兇悪な翡翠の余白に責任をもつことができるか。

downy hair has just died. The eyes of the Virgin, who is devoutly washing a cactus that is leaning against a post that is simply in line, accepts the Annunciation as if it's a rainbow. She, as much as anyone, has a floral tattoo. The emissary to the flower on the top of the tree where she can be seen is famous for soliloquies. Her latest approach is to confuse a plucked cherry blossom with a plucked lap, thereby pulling the trigger of a full moon. This allows her to finally reach that part of heaven where there is, on a chair bathed in electric-red light and swaying in the wind, the lark egg she hadn't been able to previously locate, which could be her entire universe unless it gets tired of waiting for her. It is her rising sun hidden in an empty gold can. When the soap temporarily assumes the form of Venus, she embroiders it onto the north wind by pecking and needling its uniquely melancholic eyes and ears with the beak of a baby chick. She tastes the waves from a scenic overlook. She's a producer of pine cones. She then flies straight down and is easily captured at the side of a beautiful woman. Ten million new facts sit dressed in their Sunday best in the glamour of white sand, as if they were dividends. It's nothing but a congregating flock of cranes submitting to her. It's the shipwrecking of a jet stone. How well can she catch a bird? How can she be held liable for the snow-white border of the hellacious jade?

貴下は翡翠が浴室の雪崩の上でニオベのように哭いているのを見たか?

　瓦斯はリボンを結んだ私の贈り物である。　牧草の上の王宮を見たまえ。　麦藁に興奮したまえ。　忍耐のない空の金魚すら縞撫子の靴をはく。　優美な鮫の前の胸騒ぎ。　無限の耳をもつ高慢な白鳥は雪のような美女の天才を賞美する。しかし枝振りのふしぎなギリシァの円柱のあいだで彼女の姪が朗らかな声で否定するのを聞きたまえ。　無爲の石灰または石灰の猛禽類いや夢中の麦畑それは宝石の一種である。新鮮な金属板の上の鹹い海、そこからフロマージュを要求しよう。　自発的な美人はしだいに背を曲げてもう水面に附着せんばかり。　このときようやく美人は綺麗に剃った黄菊を愛する。　白い梅は難問である。　それは妖艶な水夫に聞きたまえ。黄菊を十倍せよ。　そして巨大なヴィーナスを拝見したまえ。　彼女の黄色の狩獵に幸あれ。

Did you see the jade on the avalanche in the bathroom, like Niobe, all tears?

I have the gift of gas, tied with a ribbon. Look at the emperor's palace in the pasture. Get excited about the straw. Even the raring-to-go goldfish in the blue sky are wearing pink-striped shoes. Foreboding before an elegant shark. A proud swan with limitless hearing praises the genius of a beautiful snowlike woman. But listen to her niece happily belying it all between Greek columns with odd-shaped limbs. An idle lime or a limestone owl, no, an enraptured wheat field that's a sort of gemstone. A briny ocean on a fresh metal plate, let's ask it to serve us some *fromage*. The spontaneous beauty gradually arches her back, until she almost touches the water's surface. In that very instant, she finally falls in love with a clean-shaven yellow chrysanthemum. The white plum blossom presents some conundrums. Go ask a winsome sailor about it. Multiply the yellow chrysanthemum by ten. And look up at the enormous Venus. Good luck to her in her hunt for yellow-gold.

CHRONOLOGY OF INITIAL PUBLICATION

Note: Asterisks indicate poems not included in this volume.

LINES (June 1927)
ÉTAMINES NARRATIVES (1 July 1927; 4, 5, 6 December 1927;
    2, 3 January 1928)
amphibia (December 1927)
*basse élégie (March 1928)
Fragments (May 1928)
*The Theory of Earth's Creation (November 1928)
*The Cactus Brothers (December 1928)
The Misdeeds of Cleopatra's Daughter (January 1929)
The Flower Basket Filled with Human Death (February 1929)
TEXTE ÉVANGÉLIQUE (March 1929)
To Paul Éluard (April 1929)
DOCUMENT D'OISEAUX (July 1929)
MIROIR DE MIROIR (July 1929)
Open Letters to Mr. Sun in the Laboratory (I November 1929;
    II January 1930)
*The Royal Family of Dreams: A Manifesto, or Regarding A
    Priori Dreams (January 1930)
*TEXTES (I, II March 1930; III June 1930)
*Poetry and the Real (January 1931)
A Kiss for the Absolute (September 1931)
Stars on Earth (March 1932)
The Rock Cracked Up (September 1932)

The Sphinx in May (June 1933)
Seven Poems (October 1936)
    Salvador Dalí
    Max Ernst
    René Magritte
    Joan Miró
    Pablo Picasso
    Man Ray
    Yves Tanguy
One Thousand and One Nights on White (May 1937)
Fairy's Distance (October 1937)
    The Snail's Theatrical Stage
    Leda
    The Fish's Desire
    Snapshotting
    Undisturbed Bed Rest
    The Echo's Rose
    Reactions
    Drowsiness
    The Shadow's Passage
    Fairy's Distance
    The Conception of Wind
    Nocturne

ACKNOWLEDGMENTS

Thanks to the editors at the following magazines where these poems were published, sometimes in earlier versions:

Asymptote: "Salvador Dalí," "Max Ernst," and "Pablo Picasso"

The Awl: "Nocturne"

BBC Radio 3: "René Magritte" read by Olivia Williams on *Words and Music*—"Northern Lights: The North Pole"

Boston Review: "Document d'Oiseaux: Documenting Birds" and "Fragments"

Columbia: A Journal of Literature and Art: "Étamines Narratives"

Denver Quarterly: "Open Letters to Mr. Sun in the Laboratory"

Georgia Review: "A Kiss for the Absolute"

Gulf Coast: "Undisturbed Bed Rest"

Kenyon Review: "One Thousand and One Nights on White" and "Fairy's Distance"

LARB Quarterly Journal: "Stars on Earth"

The Literary Review: "Miroir de Miroir: Mirrored Mirror"

Oversound: "The Sphinx in May" and "Texte Évangélique"

Paris Review: "The Fish's Desire"

Poetry Magazine: "Joan Miró," "René Magritte," and "Yves Tanguy"

A Public Space: "For Paul Éluard" and "Man Ray"

RHINO: "LINES"

Riot of Perfume: "The Rock Cracked Up," "The Flower Basket
Filled with Human Death," and "The Misdeeds of Cleopa-
tra's Daughter"

Subtropics: "Leda," "Snapshotting," "Reactions," "Drowsiness,"
"The Shadow's Path," and "The Conception of Wind"

Thanks to Emily Wolahan for the "Poet to Poet" interviews on
our Takiguchi translations, which appeared in the *Two Lines Press
Journal*, Center for the Art of Translation, San Francisco.

Thanks to the editors of *RHINO Poetry*, especially Naoko Fu-
jimoto, associate editor and outreach editor for translations, for
awarding our translation of "LINES" the RHINO 2020 Transla-
tion Prize.

Thanks to the editors of *Denver Quarterly* for awarding our
translation of "Open Letters to Mr. Sun in the Laboratory" the
2020 Cole Swensen Translation Prize.

Enormous thanks to Rosanna Warren, Richard Sieburth, and
Peter Cole, the series editors of the Lockert Library of Poetry in
Translation at Princeton University Press, for their appreciation
of Takiguchi's poems and for their confidence in our translations.
Thanks to Jaden Young, our production editor, to Anne Savarese,
publisher, and everyone at the press who helped to bring this
book into the world. Our most sincere thanks to Mayumi
Kawamura for her permission to publish these poems from *The
Poetic Experiments of Shuzo Takiguchi 1927–1937*. And to Ayako
Ishigami at Misuzu Press for putting us in touch with Mayumi
Kawamura. Thanks also to Hiroaki Sato, for his Takiguchi trans-
lations, for introducing us to Miwako Tezuka, for the generous
gift of Takiguchi's fourteen-volume collected works, and espe-

cially for his friendship and support. And to Nancy Rossiter Sato. And to John Solt, whose book *Shedding the Tapestry of Meaning: The Poetry and Poetics of Kitasono Katue (1902–1978)* (Harvard East Asian Monographs, 2011) included information about Takiguchi that was helpful to us. Meeting him in Los Angeles was also extremely helpful, and much appreciated. Thanks to Miwako Tezuka, consulting curator at the ARAKAWA+GINS Reversible Destiny Foundation, for meeting to discuss the friendship between Arakawa and Takiguchi. Thanks to faculty and friends at Washington University in St. Louis, especially Ignacio Infante, David Schuman, and Kathleen Finneran. Thanks to the late Dean Young at the Michener Center. Thanks to friends, especially Timothy Donnelly, Mark Bibbins, Mónica de la Torre, Claudia Rankine, Joni Wallace, Jessica Bain, and Jennifer Kronovet. And special thanks to Eleanor Sarasohn, for her friendship, and for her expert copyediting and incisive comments on the notes. And last, but as far from least as possible, thanks to Yanbing Tan, for her help, and for her friendship.

For those who are interested in more information in English on Takiguchi, his work, and Japanese Modernism, an excellent resource is Miryam Sas's *Fault Lines: Cultural Memory and Japanese Surrealism* (Stanford University Press, 2001). Another useful work is *The Poetry and Poetics of Nishiwaki Junzaburō* (Princeton University Press, 1993); in the introduction, Hosea Hirata discusses the importance of Nishiwaki's relationship with Takiguchi. For more information about Takiguchi's writing on Surrealism and photography, a brilliant source is Jelena Stojkovic's *Surrealism and Photography in 1930s Japan: The Impossible Avant-Garde* (Routledge, 2020). The list of photography-related topics Takiguchi wrote about, noted in the introduction, is drawn from that book.

NOTES

All translations from the Japanese are by Yuki Tanaka and Mary Jo Bang, unless otherwise noted. All translations from the French are by Mary Jo Bang, unless otherwise noted.

For people's names, we elected, after much thought, to use the convention of first name first and family name second. We also chose to leave off the diacritical marks that dictate long vowel sounds in romanized Japanese. We felt they were unnecessary here since, in the few Japanese words (and names) we use, the rules of English pronunciation would dictate long vowel sounds without those marks.

LINES

This is the only poem in *The Poetic Experiments* titled in English. For more than half of the characters in this poem, Takiguchi used katakana, a method of transcription similar to italics in English and often used to transcribe foreign words into Japanese. Translating some of Takiguchi's poems in 1970s, Hiroaki Sato wrote to Takiguchi with questions. About "LINES," Takiguchi responded: "I'm not sure who began mixing in katakana or when. Surely there are previous examples of this but as far as I remember I wanted to emphasize a certain objectivity, (writing style)—writing—*écriture*, which is unique in my case. I think this became rather clear in 'The Theory of Earth's Creation' . . . became clear by comparison with other poets of the same generation. How to translate this into English (European language) is something that

should be dealt with by writing style because I wanted to empha-
size the uniqueness of Japanese by mixing in the author's subjec-
tivity. . . . But based on this premise, I'm not sure yet whether
there is any method of creating a certain kind of visual, etc, effect
in a European language. Italic? or Gothic? or—a style that uses
no capital letters?"

memories of longing for the Botticelli boy: The poem contains
echoes of Botticelli's *La Primavera* (Allegory of Spring) where
Venus, the goddess of love, beauty, passion, sex, and prostitution,
stands in the center of a grove of trees, backed by a halo of light.
Art historians note that the placement and pose of Venus echoes
depictions of the Virgin Mary and that the two female figures
were frequently conflated at the time the painting was made (ca.
1482). In *La Primavera*, the stylized lines of the red drape that
Venus holds in front of her flesh-colored dress create a distinct
dent-like V, which leads the viewer's eye to where a painter might
place a discrete fig leaf if the goddess were depicted nude. The
letter V has multiple echoes in the painting: Venus, the Virgin,
and the v of venereal—which communicates erotic love and sex-
ual desire. In the painting, above the painted Venus, a blindfolded
Cupid aims an arrow at one of the Three Graces (Aglaia, Thalia,
or Euphrosyne) who is gazing longingly toward Mars. Mars has
his back turned to the Graces and is poking at linear rain clouds
with a staff. The red-haired Graces meet in what appears to be a
dance. To the right of Venus, the nymph Chloris is transforming
into Flora, the goddess of Spring. Flowers fall from her mouth.
She is being grasped by a blue-faced Zephyrus, god of the west
wind, whose cheeks are puffed out like the image of wind on
antique maps.

Takiguchi undermines the mythology of the original painting, especially the meditative tranquility of the Venus/Virgin Mary figure, using the blindfolded, love-seeking Cupid as a stand-in for a love-seeker who hides his face in public, possibly for fear of being recognized, while the "dented" girl who "moves side to side" embodies sexual desire ("exciting purple glass, setting fire to rose petals"). Mars appears to be the poem's "Botticelli boy"; in mythology, he has a passionate affair with Venus, at least until the two are caught by Vulcan—the blacksmith god of fire to whom Venus is betrothed—and wrapped in a fine metal net.

THE MISDEEDS OF CLEOPATRA'S DAUGHTER

Cleopatra VII Philopator ruled the Ptolemaic Kingdom of Egypt from 51 to 30 BCE. She had four children, a son by Julius Caesar and a daughter and two sons by Mark Antony. The daughter, Cleopatra Selene II, married King Juba II of Numidia. They reigned over what is now Algeria.

When the marble bust opposite you burst open at the seams, you smiled a little too, didn't you: Hiroaki Sato asked Takiguchi, "Does this 'burst at the seams' mean 1) the seams unravel 2) a bud opens 3) open one's mouth and say something, or smile. Which meaning did you intend?" Takiguchi responded, " 'Get out of shape?' The meaning of the verb has changed from ancient times, and it is meant to be wholly ambiguous, with multiple meanings: burst at the seams, come untied, buds opening, smile, mouth being pried apart. I am reminded of the stripe pattern on marble. Is it possible in English to suggest the association of the stripe pattern in marble losing its shape and a face smiling?" The Japanese idiom—"The face (or mouth) comes apart at the seams"—means to smile; the face and mouth are interchangeable in the idiom. "Stripe Marble," with parallel veins of gray against a light background, comes from Greece.

This is a crane on the lake with its mouth open in a yawn: The Japanese red-crowned crane is one of the rarest of all cranes. It symbolizes good luck, longevity, and fidelity. Japanese folklore has several stories that feature cranes.

THE SPHINX IN MAY

According to Greek myth, the Sphinx is a hybrid creature—the head and torso of a woman, body of a lion, and wings of a bird— that guards the entrance to Thebes. It devours anyone who fails to answer the riddle: "What goes on four feet in the morning, two at noon, and three in the evening?" Oedipus (who unwittingly kills his father and marries his mother) solves the riddle: "Humans— they are four-footed when they crawl, two-footed when they walk, and three-footed with a cane in old age." A sphinx appears in "The Fish's Desire," as well as in Takiguchi's essay "Poetry and the Real." Riddling sphinxes were a common French Surrealist trope; in André Breton's novel, *Nadja*, Nadja lives at the Hotel Sphinx.

A KISS FOR THE ABSOLUTE

glowing like noctiluca sea sparkle: Noctiluca scintillans, commonly known as "sea sparkle," is a genus of bioluminescent marine organisms that contribute to the plankton that floats on the water's surface; in large numbers, they glow in the dark and are referred to as "blooms."

sans date: In French *sans date* means "undated."

One Thousand and One Nights is a Middle Persian, multiauthored collection of tales organized around the conceit of a fictional king (Shahryar) who, having killed his wife because of her infidelity, has his prime minister deliver him a virgin nightly. He marries each, then has her put to death in the morning. When there are only two virgins left, the prime minister's daughter, Scheherazade, volunteers in order to spare her sister. She tells the king a story each night, stopping at dawn on a cliffhanger ending. The king, eager to know how the story will progress, delays her execution. After 1001 nights, the king, having gained insight through listening to her stories, marries Scheherazade.

a danse macabre of torn shadows on a table of starving marble . . . the wind will begin to walk with a door crumbling to dust to the birthplace of umbrellas: The French *danse macabre* (dance of death) dates from the Middle Ages. It is an artistic allegorical representation of the fact that death comes to all. Typically, a parade of living figures from all socioeconomic classes, along with skeletons portraying the dead, are depicted walking together to the cemetery.

sound of a sewing machine: The combination of "a sewing machine," "the table of starving marble," and "the birthplace of umbrellas," echoes the famous line in the verse-novel *Les Chants de Maldoror* (*The Songs of Maldoror*) by Isadore Lucien Ducasse (pen name Comte de Lautréamont), who died in 1870, at the age of twenty-four. In the novel, a sixteen-year (and four months)-old British boy, "wrapped in Tartan," is described as being as beautiful as "the chance meeting on a dissecting table of a sewing machine and an umbrella." The work was rediscovered by the French Surrealists, who celebrated its wordplay, subversive sexuality, and anti-Romanticism. In 1920, Man Ray photographed a sewing machine wrapped in a blanket tied with string, titling it *L'énigma d'Isidore Ducasse* (*The Enigma of Isidore Ducasse*). André Breton quoted the line several times as a way of describing Surrealism's radical defamiliarization of the quotidian.

DOCUMENT D'OISEAUX: DOCUMENTING BIRDS
Beginning in the early 1900s, the Pathé Frères (Pathé Brothers) film company made multiple short documentary films about birds. We opted to use the word "documentary," instead of "document," in the final sentence of the poem—based on the fact that the French word for a documentary film, *documentaire*, is often abbreviated in conversation to *document*. Additionally, the Muse is having makeup applied, as would be the case if she were in a film.

the Koi star cluster: The koi is a type of carp fish that symbolizes good luck and abundance. The constellation Pisces is similarly "the fish." Another Japanese *koi* (恋) means romantic love or lust. To re-create the wordplay, instead of "constellation," we chose "star cluster," which has lust embedded in it.

the trunk of a Greek fir tree again conceives an Apollo: When Apollo's lover, Cyparissus, was inconsolable after accidentally killing his pet stag, Apollo turned him into a cone-bearing cypress tree, the symbol of mourning.

On the paramount seashore, a cigar is burning: The Japanese word 至上 translates as highest, supreme, or paramount. We chose "paramount" to gesture to the film studio Paramount Pictures, which was founded in 1914.

That white world was neither an isle nor an ibis: Takiguchi uses 鳥, the general character for bird, pairing it with the visually similar character for island or isle 島. We chose to translate the bird as an ibis, a white bird found in coastal areas, and pair it with isle as a way to re-create the visual similarity of the Japanese. In English, "isle" and "ibis" are additionally tied together by the long "i" sound.

Because I stole a glance at a god sculpting a peach, I die: In Chinese mythology, peaches confer immortality on the deities who eat them. In Chinese art, they symbolize the wish for a long life.

the lion trumpets the spring with his beautiful voice: Beginning in 1916, Leo the Lion was the Goldwyn Pictures logo. The company was later subsumed into Metro-Goldwyn-Mayer (MGM), which continued to use Leo's image and now made him roar. In the 1920s, the lion was sometimes pictured in a blue circle.

Outside, lovebirds are twittering during The Four Seasons: Vivaldi's *Le quartto stagioni* (The Four Seasons) is a set of four violin concertos, each representing a different season. Vivaldi radically incorporated actual birdsong, as well as barking dogs, fires, storms, and other sounds into the music. Takiguchi's "four seasons" (四季) is used in Japanese for the Vivaldi title as well as for the four natural divisions of the year. We have capitalized and italicized the term to better gesture to the music.

This poem also has echoes of Botticelli's *La Primavera* (Allegory of Spring); both the poem and the painting share Venus, Mars (Roman: Mercury), and hyacinths. Other elements in the poem mirror elements of Botticelli's *The Birth of Venus*, which features a youthful Venus with a long neck and prominent white fingers, the inside of a shell, and reeds.

danse des impuissants de la création: The epigraph is a fragment of a line from Tristan Tzara's 1918 *Manifeste Dada* (*Dada Manifesto*). The entire line reads: "*DADA; abolition de la logique, danse des impuissants de la création*," which translates as: "DADA; abolishment of logic, the dance of those powerless to create."

On my finger is a gunmetal-gray Ruby: Takiguchi has "gray ruby." We have modified gray with "gunmetal" and capitalized Ruby to gesture to the then well-known Ruby pistol, *Pistolet Automatique de 7 millim.65 genre "Ruby,"* a Spanish-manufactured, semi-automatic firearm used by the French during World War I. The barrel of the gun was gunmetal gray.

An exact Beaufort-3 breeze lasts for three days: The Beaufort wind force scale—devised by Irish Royal Naval officer Frances Beaufort—is a measurement of wind speed that has been in existence since 1805. Originally a way of measuring the effect of wind on sails, today, a level 3 on the Beaufort scale is described as a "gentle breeze," which is what Takiguchi wrote.

ÉTAMINES NARRATIVES

Takiguchi gave this poem only a French title. In French, the word *étamine* has two distinct meanings: (1) stamen, the reproductive part of a plant consisting of thread-like filaments with pollen-containing anthers at their tips; and (2) the individual threads that are woven together to form flax linen fabric. The word "line," as in "poetic lines," comes from the same "linen." An English translation could be "The Stamen's Narrative Threads."

a mole spilling its chlorophyll: The "mole" mentioned here is the small, velvety, burrowing mammal of the family Talpidae. Another "mole" is the unit of measurement in chemistry used to express the molar mass of chlorophyll (on average, 900 grams per mole); that word is the same in English, French, and Japanese. In English, there are, of course, two other "moles," the pigmented nevus and the counterespionage agent (an undercover "plant") that works from within the organization. Takiguchi includes both the mammalian mole and the mole that is a pigmented nevus in several poems. The word "mole" appears eight times in *The Poetic Experiments.*

STARS ON EARTH

a verse as old as a Tibetan temple: The word 詩, meaning verse or poetry, is made up of 言 (word) and 寺 (temple). Takiguchi creates a pun on the word 詩 by comparing it to a "Tibetan temple." To replicate the wordplay, we translated the third 詩 in these lines as "word temple": "I write a verse as old as a Tibetan temple / Then tear it to pieces / I write a verse / I write a word temple."

O valley in Vallon: In French, *vallon* means "a small valley." There is a village in Southern France, *Vallon-Pont-d'Arc*, which takes its name from the *Pont d'Arc*, a tall natural arch at the entrance to the Ardèche canyon.

The lace DENTELLE of the fairy of the Forever Festival, of the festival of this moment, dances in my heart like a kite: Dentelle is the French word for "lace." Belgian "Binche lace," woven in two-inch strips, is known as "fairy lace." The "kite" in the poem is the bird, not the frame covered in fabric or paper and flown at the end of a string. The wordplay between the homophonic bird / kite and plaything / kite possibly anticipates a reader who knows English. Additionally, the combination of the "DENT" and "ELLE" in the French *dentelle* (*dent* is tooth; *elle* is she or her) echoes the "dented girl" in the poem "LINES"; for a reader who knows both French and English, it might also suggest a *fée des dents*, or "tooth fairy."

the French manucure: Takiguchi uses the French word *manucure*, which means both "manicure" and "manicurist."

Les Illuminations is a reed: Les Illuminations, a group of prose poems written by Arthur Rimbaud, was published in 1886 by Publications de la Vogue. The title was suggested by his former lover, Paul Verlaine, who said Rimbaud had used it as a subtitle. An "illuminé" is a visionary; thus one could think of these illuminations as visions.

ÉVENTAIL D'INTELLIGENCE: Éventail is French for "range, spectrum, or fan." *Intelligence*, a cognate, means intelligence. The phrase can be translated as "range of intelligence."

*an astounding concurrence of rainbows * * *:* Takiguchi uses the word "rainbow" (虹) nineteen times in *The Poetic Experiments.*

Like a shrunken young Télémaque: François Fénelon, a Catholic archbishop and tutor to the seven-year-old grandson of Louis XIV (Louis-Auguste, who would become Louis XVI, the last monarch before the French Revolution), published *Les aventures de Télémaque* (*The Adventures of Telemachus*) anonymously in 1699 as an Enlightenment argument against the excesses of the aristocracy. In it, a tutor named Mentor travels with Telemachus, the son of Ulysses in the Odyssey. At the story's end, Mentor is revealed to be Minerva, the Roman goddess of wisdom. In 1922, the Surrealist poet Louis Aragon published a parody of the Fénelon book, also titled *Les aventures de Télémaque.*

the lacquer-master's lamb discovered her mouth on a snow-white cylinder: The "lacquer master" may be Thomas Edison, credited with inventing the phonograph record. The first pressed cylinder, made in 1878, featured Edison reciting the nursery rhyme, "Mary Had a Little Lamb," which begins "Mary had a little lamb, / Its fleece was white as snow." Early phonograph records were manufactured by cutting a master disc or lacquer. Those who cut them were called "lacquer masters." Takiguchi's Japanese word, however, refers to the artists called "lacquer masters" who practiced the well-established decorative art of applying lacquer to a wide range of objects (lacquerware). Japanese readers would surely have thought of those artists and not of Edison. It is only the lamb who finds her mouth on the pure-white cylinder, combined with an apparent reference to Edison as "the great hero of the fluoroscopic image" in "The Royal Family of Dreams: A Manifesto, or

Regarding A Priori Dreams" (not included in this selection), that makes a secondary reading possible.

A red throat was foretold. This wouldn't trouble anyone but colorists: Takiguchi uses the word 色彩家, a colorist or "one who deals with color," a term usually applied to painters skilled in using color but not limited to them. Johann Wolfgang von Goethe was a color theorist. Goethe's book, *Zur Farbenlehre* (On Color Theory), was published in 1810. *Faust I* was translated into Japanese by Goro Takahashi in 1904; a complete *Faust* translation by Mori Ogai was published in 1913. From *Faust* (trans. James Stewart Blackie): "*Soldiers.* From the red throat of death, / With the spear and the glave, / We pluck the ripe glory, / That blooms for the brave."

Although they had dreamed of a billion kinds of cypresses, just now the memory of one drop of gold liquid rose up: Goethe, *Faust* (trans. James Stewart Blackie): "*Faust.* Or liquid gold that instantly will melt and run / Like quicksilver between my fingers / A game that no one's ever won."

A wild-parsley room: Thomas Mann's 1924 novel *Der Zauberberg* (*The Magic Mountain*) shares a number of words with this section of "Mr. Sun". One of them is parsley. In that work, Hans Castorp leaves Hamburg to visit his cousin in a tuberculosis sanatorium in the Swiss Alps near the Scaletta Glacier. In the novel, there are "dishes of delectables, all garnished with little radishes, butter-balls, and parsley, gay as flower-beds"; there is also an allusion to Japan in the novel via the description of a newsreel seen at a cinema—"geishas sitting behind seven wooden lattices." Other unusual words that occur in both the novel and in Takiguchi's poem are celadon, quicksilver (or mercury), saliva, glacier, a golden eagle, Wednesday, sacrilegious, soprano, semicircular, eye socket, omnipotence, airless, purse, diamonds, Platonic, arctic, sleeves—as well as many common ones like laboratory, crimson, hand, wing, landscape, lightning, secrets, ladle, needle, instrument, and countless others. The novel was translated into English by Helen Tracy Lowe-Porter and published in 1927 in the United States by Alfred A. Knopf and in England by Martin Secker.

The novel alpine mountain and its strange glacier: Takiguchi uses 新 (new, novel, original) to describe the alp. We have used "novel" for new expressly for the pun it creates in English and the hope that the punning will further gesture to Mann's novel. The association between novel meaning new (新) and novel meaning a work of fiction (小説) does not exist in Japanese. In the novel, the Scaletta Glacier is described as glowing ice-blue. The surrealist poet Paul Éluard was hospitalized in the same tuberculosis sanatorium (Clavadel in Davos) from 1912 to 1914.

nor does it necessarily need the Pyrenees: The mountain range known as the Pyrenees defines the border between France and Spain. The Pyrenees is mentioned twice in Thomas Mann's *The Magic Mountain*. A famous quote from Blaise Pascal's *Pensées* (*Thoughts*) speaks to the fact that the chain acts as a cultural dividing line—"Vérité en deçà des Pyrénées, erreur au delà" ("Truth on this side of the Pyrenees, error on the other")—that is, what's right over here is wrong over there.

On your favorite silk horse, you encounter an amethyst Tengu goblin: The Japanese *Tengu*, literally "heavenly dog," is a supernatural creature that ranges in representation from an enormous bird with a long beak to a human-like goblin with a red face and large nose.

The moment you climbed up on the ship's tossed deck, the starry night splashed you with latest Platonist's sea spray: After discovering the reiterative use of the word "Platonist" in Herman Melville's *Moby-Dick; or, The Whale*, we added the word "tossed" to Takiguchi's "ship's deck": "[T]here floated a little isle of sunlight, from which beamed forth an angel's face; and this bright face shed a distant spot of radiance upon the ship's tossed deck." In the novel, Captain Ahab pursues a white whale into the Sea of Japan and is defeated by it just off the coast, near where the white whale had previously bitten off his leg. A "Platonist" appears twice: "Beware of . . . any lad with lean brow and hollow eye; given to unseasonable meditativeness. . . . [T]his sunken-eyed young Platonist will tow you ten wakes round the world, and never make you one pint of sperm the richer. . . . [T]hose young Platonists have a notion that their vision is imperfect; they are short-sighted; what use, then, to strain the visual nerve? They have left their opera-glasses at home."

The time for allegories has already passed: Moby Dick is presumably one of those allegories whose time has already passed. The novel was published in 1851.

SEVEN POEMS
The titles of these seven poems—"Salvador Dalí," "Max Ernst," "René Magritte," "Joan Miró," "Pablo Picasso," "Man Ray," and "Yves Tanguy"—are the names of surrealist painters. The poems were published in the October 1936 issue of *L'Échange surréaliste*

(*The Surrealist Exchange*), which also included work by Éluard and Breton, translated into Japanese prior to being published in French (Miryam Sas, *Fault Lines: Cultural Memory and Japanese Surrealism*, Stanford, CA: Stanford University Press, 1999, pp. 25–26).

SALVADOR DALÍ
This poem contains multiple echoes of elements found in Dalí's charcoal-and-white-chalk drawing, *Le piano surréaliste* (The Surrealist Piano): a huge "zipper-bag" piano, a mysterious eroded shoreline at the edge of the piano, a headless woman with a clock for a face, and Dalí's signature along the lower-left edge. The drawing was reportedly done in 1937, while Dalí was working on the set of the Marx Brother's film *A Day at the Races*. Given that the poem was published in November 1936, and filming in the United States only began in late September of the same year, it seems impossible that Takiguchi could have seen the drawing. The echoes appear to be an odd surrealist coincidence.

THE FLOWER BASKET FILLED WITH HUMAN DEATH
Venus's Flower Basket (*Euplectella aspergillum*) is a latticework, vase-shaped Asian sea sponge composed of silica fibers. Shrimp-like creatures called decapods breed inside the sponge; the offspring leave, but the parents outgrow the exit and must remain until death. For this reason, the dried basket, representing the phrase, "Till death do us part," is sometimes given as a wedding gift in Japan.

The Goddess of Beauty swims toward the horizon of my fingers:
Venus, the Roman Goddess of Beauty associated with sex, love,

and fertility (Greek: Aphrodite), was said to have been born from sea foam after Cronus castrated his father Uranus, the Sky, and threw his genitals into the sea.

If this is the triumphal arch of a disease-free human, let a blast of wind blow against this mons's Mont Blanc, as if it were a windmill: Mont Blanc is the highest peak in the Alps. The mons is the rounded fatty protuberance below the pubic arch.

one of the Muses has grown cold: In Greek mythology, there were nine Muses.

In the deep sea, wearing a speedy locomotive, I roll a blue-dyed Venus in a hallway: In the Roman dice game of knucklebones, the luckiest roll of the dice, worth fourteen points, was called a "Venus Throw."

the olive flounder's David-like profile: The original Japanese indicates that this is King David from the Old Testament. The small pelvic fin on the ventral aspect of the olive flounder (also known as the bastard halibut) resembles a beard.

the bright idea that lignite would make quite a nice match: Lignite is a form of wood coal.

AMPHIBIA

Takiguchi titled this poem with the Latin word *amphibia* (English: amphibious), from the ancient Greek ἀμφίβιος (amphíbios), which means "living a double life." The *amphibia* class of vertebrates includes frogs, toads, salamanders, and burrowing earth-worm-like caecilians, all of which are born and bred in water but primarily live on land as adults.

the golden-hamlet-fish refused to say yes to dying: The golden hamlet fish, *Hypoplectrus gummigutta*, was identified in 1851 by the Cuban zoologist Felipe Poey. The fish are hermaphroditic, having both male and female sex organs. During mating, the two fish take turns playing the role of male or female. We added the "hamlet" to the "golden fish" who "refused to say yes to dying" based on the fact that there are other subtle allusions to Shakespeare's *Hamlet* in other poems.

his convertible-collar's clear weather: We added "convertible" to "collar"; a convertible collar can be worn either open or closed, which echoes the idea of the "double life" that is inherent in the title.

TO PAUL ÉLUARD

Eugène Émile Paul Grindel (1895–1952) was a French Surrealist poet known as Paul Éluard. Takiguchi quotes from Éluard poems in both "Poetry and the Real" and in "The Royal Family of Dreams: A Manifesto, or Regarding A Priori Dreams."

MIROIR DE MIROIR: MIRRORED MIRROR

In Jacob and Wilhelm Grimm's tale *Snow White* (*Schneewittchen*), each day Snow White's vain stepmother asks her magic mirror, "Mirror, mirror, on the wall, who is the fairest of them all?" There are also seven dwarfs in the story of *Snow White* and "seven perfect natures" in the poem. The word "mirror" is a playful element for Takiguchi; it appears over forty times in *The Poetic Experi-*

ments. In this poem, the title mirrors the word "mirror" in French and in the English translation; the word then occurs eight more times in the body of the poem. A mirror inside a mirror was the cover image of the monograph *Fairy's Distance*, line drawings by the painter Yoshibumi Abe, with poems by Takiguchi (see the note to "Fairy's Distance").

what is that light bulb shining most brightly above the ninth girl's eyebrows: The ninth muse, Urania, was associated with astronomy and is often pictured holding a globe and a compass.

A vision of wheat fields: Not only is the poem titled in French but it also incorporates the French word OUI (all caps in the original), meaning "yes." The poem emphasizes numbers: the ninth girl's eyebrows; Zero's peacock; seven mirrors; four sides; one celestial body; one sign; seven perfect natures on the lake; (1) ruby; (2) marble knees. These last two are given in numerical form in the original, which further emphasizes numbers. Takiguchi uses the word "wheat" four times in the poem. In French, the word for the number eight is *huit*, a homophone of English "wheat."

The white rapids demolish the memorial Hydrangea statue, the latest lovefest: Amacha (sweet tea), made from the leaves of the hydrangea, is poured over statues of Buddha on April 8, the date believed to be his birthday. According to legend, nine dragons poured this tea over him when he was born. Hydrangeas are associated with heartfelt emotions but can also represent boastfulness.

THE ROCK CRACKED UP

beneath Ryogoku Bridge: Since the early 1900s, Ryogoku, a district in Tokyo, has been the center of professional sumo wrestling. The word *ryogoku* means "two provinces." The Ryogoku Bridge, which spans the Sumida River, was built in 1659 to connect Edo Province and Shimosa Province.

FAIRY'S DISTANCE

The twelve poems in this series—"The Snail's Theatrical Stage," "Leda," "The Fish's Desire," "Snapshotting," "Undisturbed Bed Rest," "The Echo's Rose," "Reactions," "Drowsiness," "The Shadow's Passage," "Fairy's Distance," "The Conception of Wind," and "Nocturne"—are ekphrastic responses to abstract monochrome illustrations by the artist/photographer Yoshibumi Abe. The sequence was published with the drawings in 1937 as *Yosei no kyori* (Fairy's Distance). The cover image was a photograph of a small hand mirror inside a larger hand mirror (a "mirrored mirror").

Yosei no kyori (Fairy's Distance), poems by
Shuzo Takiguchi, illustrations by Yoshibumi Abe

THE SNAIL'S THEATRICAL STAGE

Triton's quieted fountain: The Greek god Triton was the son of the sea god and goddess, Poseidon and Amphitrite. He was often represented as a merman—a human upper body ending in a fish tail. He usually carries both a trident and a twisted conch shell. When he blew the conch shell, the noise was said to be so loud it raised the waves.

LEDA

In Greek myth, Leda is the queen of Sparta and mother of Helen of Troy (who hatched from an egg). When Leda comforts Zeus—who has taken the form of a swan and is fleeing an eagle—he impregnates her. Leda appears in "Stars on Earth" and in this eponymous poem, where she is "left hanging"—perhaps by her straight pin, which is said in the poem to be "taking a rest."

THE FISH'S DESIRE

subtle sphinx of love: We added the word "subtle," suggested by Shakespeare's *Love's Labour's Lost*: "Subtle as Sphinx; as sweet and musical / As bright Apollo's lute, strung with his hair" (IV. iii.318–319).

UNDISTURBED BED REST

An infantile moth bears the weight of night's mammoth bottle: Atlas moths, endemic to Asian shrubland and forests, can have a wingspan of up to ten inches. In Greek myth, Atlas was a Titan tasked with holding up the sky.

THE ECHO'S ROSE

an echo of O arose from the ash: In Japanese folklore, *kodama* were spirits that resided in trees, similar to the dryads or wood nymphs in Greek myths. *Kodama* is also used in Japanese for "echo," which is said to be the plaintive cry the *kodama* makes when an axe chops into a tree or a tree falls in the forest.

THE CONCEPTION OF WIND
Your salad days are shaken up / by the mammoth hinge of night:
For 若さ (youth), we used "salad days," a synonym for youth derived from Shakespeare's *Antony and Cleopatra*: "My salad days, / When I was green in judgement, cold in blood" (I.v.73–74).

TEXTE ÉVANGÉLIQUE
The French title can be translated either as "Evangelical Text," or as "Gospel Text." Takiguchi appears to again playfully fuse Venus—the goddess of beauty seen on a half-shell in Botticelli's *Nascita di Venere* (The Birth of Venus)—with the evangelical Virgin Mary. The pentagram is a five-sided star pattern associated with Venus (both the planet—because its transit over the course of eight earth-years, relative to the sun, forms a pentagon inside a circle—and the goddess). The "true virgin" chooses the dove-like Holy Spirit, thus rendering obsolete the Apollonian/Dionysian male partner. Venus, on the other hand, appears to give up her virginity. Afterward, she regretfully reimagines the deflowering and sheds tears, while outside, under a seductive moon, a choir of grateful phallic cucumbers cheers the errant ways of fallen virgins. In the painting, Venus is offered a modesty drape by a clothed double, a post-virginal Hora of Spring who wears a flowered empire-style dress and a garland of leaves—possibly the poem's "holy bonbons." In the poem, the diaphanous dress restores the appearance of innocence as much as a fig leaf, or a

mirror made out of mist. In the Botticelli painting, the naked goddess's left hand is placed exactly where one frequently finds a fig leaf in religious depictions of Adam and Eve after the fall.

Did you see the jade on the avalanche in the bathroom, like Niobe, all tears: Jade, as outdated slang, can refer to a worn-out horse or a "promiscuous" woman. Niobe is a figure from Greek mythology who, after the murder of her seven sons and seven daughters, fled to Mount Sipylus, where she was turned into a perpetually weeping rock face. In Shakespeare's *Hamlet: Prince of Denmark*, Hamlet uses the trope of Niobe to describe his widowed mother (the Queen), " . . . she followed my poor father's body / Like Niobe, all tears . . . / O God, a beast that wants discourse with reason / Would have mourned longer—" (I.ii.148–151).

let's ask it to serve us some fromage: Takiguchi uses the French. There is a French idiom, *en faire un fromage*, literally "make a cheese out of it," which figuratively means to make a fuss over something trivial, as in "to make a mountain out of a molehill."

THE LOCKERT LIBRARY OF POETRY IN TRANSLATION

Final Matters: Selected Poems, 2004–2010, by Szilárd Borbély, translated by Ottilie Mulzet

Selected Poems of Giovanni Pascoli, translated by Taije Silverman with Marina Della Putta Johnston

After Callimachus: Poems, by Stephanie Burt, with a foreword by Mark Payne

Dear Ms. Schubert: Poems by Ewa Lipska, translated by Robin Davidson and Ewa Elżbieta Nowakowska, with a foreword by Adam Zagajewski

The Translator of Desires, by Muhyiddin Ibn ʿArabi, translated by Michael Sells

Cantigas: Galician-Portuguese Troubadour Poems, translated and introduced by Richard Zenith

The Owl and the Nightingale: A New Verse Translation, translated by Simon Armitage

Brief Homage to Pluto, by Fabio Pusterla, selected and translated by Will Schutt

A Kiss for the Absolute: Selected Poems of Shuzo Takiguchi, translated by Mary Jo Bang and Yuki Tanaka

† Out of print

Printed in the USA
CPSIA information can be obtained
at www.ICGtesting.com
JSHW020742170924
69849JS00003B/4